TAKE CHARGE OF YOU

IDEAPRESS
PUBLISHING

"*Take Charge of You* offers a unique combination of activities that will guide you through an empowering self-coaching process. Get ready to become more self-aware and learn how to occupy your mind with relevant information on the way to achieving your biggest goals."

—MIA HAMM, Professional Soccer Player, Two-Time World Cup
Winner, and Olympic Gold Medalist

"This book, from two of the most important coaches of our time, will teach you everything about peak performance and peak living. Read it carefully and follow the advice to be in flow."

—DEEPAK CHOPRA, MD

"In a time of distraction and comparison, it's more critical than ever to commit to the art of self-coaching. More than just to inform or teach, this book empowers you with the resources you need to go beyond and build the life you're meant to live so that you can give your best to the world. Consider this your cheat sheet on how to shine your brightest in both your personal and professional lives."

—KENDRA SCOTT, Founder of Kendra Scott, LLC

"An excellent read! David and Jason have partnered to share key lessons learned that will benefit all of their readers. *Take Charge of You* provides a simple and practical path for continued personal development."

—BRIAN CORNELL, CEO, Target

"Most of the success I've had in my career I owe to a lifetime of learning from people who have taught me so many invaluable lessons. But I also have no doubt that mental toughness and knowing how to coach myself has become critical to my personal and professional growth over the past twenty years, and this book will teach you how to do just that in your life. Good luck on your journey."

—TOM BRADY, NFL Quarterback and Seven-Time Super Bowl Winner

"David and Jason distill their years of leadership and coaching experience in an entertaining and immediately useful guide to your future. For anyone who's ever felt stuck in a career or life path, this supremely practical and evidence-based book will take you from dreaming to doing."

—MARGARET DUFFY, PhD, Professor of Strategic Communication, University of Missouri

"Throughout my football career, I've benefited from many coaches surrounding me. However, off the field, I've often had to teach myself different ways to lead and work. David and Jason's book taught me a framework to coach myself on my own personal growth and development journey."

—LARRY FITZGERALD, Retired NFL Wide Receiver

"*Take Charge of You* is an inspiring and insightful guide to achieving one's personal and professional goals. It provides many effective exercises to help clarify goals and then identify what is standing in the way of achieving them. It helps clear obstacles with the power of positive thinking and reframing of the challenge. Throughout the book, David and Jason share many personal obstacles that they have been through and overcome, making the learnings real and practical. A great book for anyone working to further their personal development!"

— **LAUREN HOBART**, President and CEO, Dick's Sporting Goods

"David and Jason lay out a no-nonsense blueprint for self-coaching to help you better understand yourself, what motivates you, and what it takes to be a real leader. David truly set the standard for all business leaders—not only in his emphasis on teamwork and management development but also in his deep integrity and strategic vision. This book draws on success stories from leaders across various fields, demonstrating the importance of continuous self-improvement—and why humility should always serve as your guide."

— **JAMIE DIMON**, Chairman and CEO, JPMorgan Chase

"Jason and David collaborating on *Take Charge of You* ... home run, and a must-read. From my perspective, Jason Goldsmith is the best mind/body coach in sports. He has a gift for helping athletes of any age to manage competitive stress and anxiety and how to focus and compete in the moment. And if there was a business Hall of Fame, David would be a first-ballot inductee."

— **TOM HOUSE**, PhD, Cofounder, Mustard

"It's hard to overstate how transformative self-coaching can be on your outlook and performance. From practical steps like tackling stage fright to the more profound questions about purpose and meaning, the methods in this book will show you how to stop worrying, how to stop settling for less, and how to start truly living."

—ED MACARTHUR, Actor, Comedian, and Educator

"*Take Charge of You* is an excellent resource for anyone looking to achieve their best in life as well as leaders out there looking to make an impact in others' lives. This book will give you practical tools and tips for obtaining growth personally and professionally. Coaching helped me achieve milestones professionally I never thought possible, and self-coaching is critical for constantly resetting the bar higher in life."

—ERIC WOOD, Former NFL Center, Buffalo Bills

TAKE CHARGE OF YOU

HOW SELF-COACHING CAN TRANSFORM *YOUR* LIFE AND CAREER

• • • • • • • •

DAVID NOVAK
JASON GOLDSMITH

IDEAPRESS
PUBLISHING

WASHINGTON, D.C.

IDEAPRESS
PUBLISHING

Proudly printed in the United States of America by Ideapress Publishing.

Ideapress Publishing | **www.ideapresspublishing.com**

David Novak has donated all net income he would have received from the sale of this book to David Novak Leadership, Inc., a Section 501(c)(3) charity whose mission is to make the world a better place by developing better leaders at every stage of life. We believe that the world needs better leaders and that everyone has it in them to lead. It's never too early—nor too late—to learn how to lead others in an uplifting and collaborative way to accomplish big goals and meet today's greatest challenges.

Cover Design by Molly von Borstel, Faceout Studios
Interior Design by Paul Nielsen, Faceout Studios
Icon Design by Cliff Hilton, David Novak Leadership

Cataloging-in-Publication Data is on file with the Library of Congress.

ISBN: 978-1-64687-0615

SPECIAL SALES

Ideapress books are available at a special discount for bulk purchases for sales promotions or corporate training programs. Special editions, including personalized covers and custom forewords, are also available. For more details, contact the author directly at info@davidnovakleadership.com.

Dedicated to YOU ...
the best coach you'll ever have.

CONTENTS

INTRODUCTION TO SELF-COACHING

Becoming the Best *You* You Can Be

Everyone wants to find success in their life and career. The question is how to get there. Well, this book is going to show you a way that not many coaches will tell you about. It's going to show you how you can *coach yourself* to success.

A few years ago, Google created Project Oxygen with the purpose of discovering what makes someone a good manager—or determining if managers even matter for success. Team members went to work gathering and analyzing data and came up with a definite conclusion: Not only do managers matter a lot, but the best ones display a consistent set of eight traits. Can you guess what was number one on the list—the most important quality successful managers should have? First and foremost, good managers are good coaches.[1]

Of course that shouldn't come as a surprise. The importance of good coaching has been studied and written about for some time now. It can help people see themselves and their experiences more clearly. It can help them respond to situations more effectively. It can help them expand their knowledge and capabilities. It can help them define what they need to do and stay on track as they do it. In short, good coaching can help them reach more of their potential and become the best they can be.

Yet, despite all the known benefits, good coaching doesn't seem to be practiced all that much. Following up on his identification of six defining leadership styles, Daniel Goleman, psychologist and author of the bestselling *Emotional Intelligence*, wrote that even though coaching has been shown to improve results, "the coaching style is used *least often* [among the six leadership styles] in our high-pressure economy."[2]

Where does that leave all the people out there in need of a good coach?

The need is clear. How many times have we heard how disengaged people are at work? The Gallup numbers come out every year and they never seem to budge all that much. According to Gallup's recent *State of the Global Workplace* report, 85% of employees are not engaged, or worse, are actively disengaged at work.[3] That means there are a lot of people out there who just don't like their jobs, despite the fact that they spend at least a quarter of their time at work.

Americans are also starting new businesses at the fastest rate in more than a decade,[4] and they are opting for freelance or gig work more and more often.[5] And they are increasingly working from home, which means they are likely without a manager or mentor on hand to act as their coach. People in these kinds of situations often don't have options for personal coaching without paying high prices for it. Whether you work for yourself or for someone else, the market is becoming increasingly competitive and dynamic—if you don't know how to develop yourself and your skills, you will fall behind.

So what are people who want to grow and achieve more supposed to do? Are they supposed to sit around and hope that their organizations get with the program? Are they supposed to wait and see if their bosses develop the coaching skills they need to succeed? And what about all the people who are self-employed, have lost a job, are transitioning to new careers, or retiring? It's often in those transitional moments, whether professional or personal (i.e., moving to a new town, deciding whether to start a family, recovering from grief or illness) when people need coaching the most. But so often those are the moments when we end up having to figure things out on our own. Where are people who find themselves in these kinds of situations supposed to find the coaching help they could sorely use?

As important as coaches are, there just aren't enough good ones to go around—in fact, there's a real coaching deficit out there. And the coaches who do exist are often far too expensive and in too high demand for most people to consider hiring their own. But that doesn't mean you should go without. Your life is too important to leave your personal growth and professional development to chance. It's time to take the responsibility for coaching into your own hands and give yourself what you need to succeed, grow, and lead a more fulfilling life. It's time to *take charge of you* and learn how to self-coach.

● ● ● ● ● ● ● ●

Coaching yourself doesn't mean that you have to go it alone and can't look to others for help or guidance. Quite the opposite. It means you are constantly looking for ways to grow yourself and for anything and anyone who can help you do that.

We want to provide that help for you and be your guides on your self-coaching journey. We know we can because we have many decades of coaching experience between us, and we have helped thousands of people transform their lives and careers. We know how to coach others, and we know how to coach ourselves. Our backgrounds enable us to provide a combination of business, performance, and life-coaching skills that you can't find anywhere else.

We first met because, even at this later stage of our careers, we found reason to seek out coaching from each other. In the beginning, David was simply looking for help with his golf game. Jason's performance coaching fundamentally changed it for the better, and then our relationship started working the other way around, too. We got to know each other and became close friends, and that was when David started using his coaching expertise to help Jason build his business.

Along the way, we discovered something: There were basic things we both did that were coaching essentials—it didn't matter whether it was in an office or on a golf course. We also realized that having coaching skills—especially self-coaching skills—has benefited us both in countless ways. It has helped our careers, of course, but it has also been invaluable in improving just about every aspect of our lives.

• • • • • • • •

David: In 1997 I was working at PepsiCo, heading up two of its three restaurant brands, KFC and Pizza Hut, when a decision was made to spin-off the company's restaurants to create an entirely new company. The decision had been a well-kept secret, so when Roger Enrico, PepsiCo's CEO, called me into his office to tell me the news, I was caught by surprise. I was even more surprised—and not in a good way—when he told me I was going to be "co-leader" of the new company along with the head of PepsiCo's third restaurant brand, Taco Bell.

"Co-leader" wasn't exactly what it sounded like. The other guy was going to be named CEO, while I would be president and second in command. Something about the idea didn't sit right with me, but I didn't say anything right away. And I couldn't ask anyone for advice. The new management team was to remain a secret until PepsiCo was ready to announce it publicly, which meant I had to navigate the situation on my own.

I figured I had to give Enrico's idea a chance. The head of Taco Bell was relatively new to his position, so I suggested we meet for dinner to get to know each other better. When Enrico pitched the co-leader idea to me, he had positioned this guy as having more financial capability than I did, which was why he would be CEO and I would be his second. But as we talked, I discovered that wasn't really true. He had previously worked at a convenience store chain and been part of the management team that brought the company out of Chapter 11. But I learned that his role had been in operations, while someone else oversaw the financial side. There were other things that gnawed at me, too. He didn't have as much experience as I did in the restaurant business, and he didn't seem to share my passion for it, either. He was more interested in talking about the money we would make. We had different backgrounds, but by the end of our conversation, I was convinced I could do the job just as well as he could—if not a whole lot better.

Of course it's one thing for me to think that. It's another to get other people to agree. After the meeting, I started working on ways to convince Enrico that I should get the top job instead. Enrico wasn't happy that I hadn't accepted his co-leader offer right away, and word got back to him that I was working on other options. Not long after, I got a call from the head of HR.

"David, if you're not careful, you're going to get fired," he told me.

"If you guys want to fire me, then go ahead and fire me," I shot back.

I was upset and my response reflected it. As soon as I hung up, I realized I was in deep trouble. If you go up against the boss, only one person wins and it isn't you. I knew if I was going to get what I wanted, I needed to approach things with a different mindset.

I knew Enrico didn't want to fire me. He valued my expertise, and besides that we were friends. But I needed to smooth things over, and to do that, I needed to let him know how much I appreciated all the things that he'd done for me. I also needed to show him that if he had to choose between the head of Taco Bell and me, I was the obvious choice. So I put together a thirty-page presentation and set up a meeting.

It was a holiday when we met, and everyone had the day off, leaving the office oddly quiet. I began by apologizing to Enrico for acting so emotionally and explaining that I had done so because the situation wasn't sitting right in my heart. He knew I was a passionate person, so he accepted that. And that allowed me to make my case.

At the end of my presentation I said to Enrico, "Okay, you don't think I can be CEO. I think I can, but I'll accept that I don't have as much financial experience as you'd like. So all I ask is that you give me someone I can learn from." I suggested a few names of people who, in my opinion, would be stronger CEOs than the head of Taco Bell. One of them was Andy Pearson, a former president of PepsiCo and renowned professor at Harvard Business School. I knew that Pearson had a deep well of experience, which would complement my own, and that, at the age of seventy-two, he would be ready to let me take the reins sooner rather than later. Enrico listened and agreed. Pearson came on board as CEO, and I accepted the position of president. What's more, Pearson became one of my closest friends and allies. Even though he had a three-year contract as CEO, he stepped aside after we had worked together for just two years. That's when I was named CEO of Yum! Brands, the largest restaurant company in the world.

This might never have happened if I hadn't been able to coach myself through that crucial moment. I could have blown it so easily. When the head of HR told me I could get fired, he wasn't kidding. That's how angry Enrico was at me.

It might sound strange, but years later, after I retired from my position as CEO, I used similar skills to coach myself through a cancer diagnosis. It's a story I'll talk more about later in this book, but I mention it now because self-coaching really helped me through it. It helped me accept the reality of the situation and humbly admit that so much of it was outside my control—but also to realize that I wasn't completely powerless. With that mindset, I was able to step back and decide what I wanted to happen, and learn everything I could about how to give myself the best chance of surviving. Then I worked toward that, through good days and bad, until I was in remission.

● ● ● ● ● ● ● ●

Jason: I have been a professional performance coach working with top athletes for more than eleven years now. I have found real joy and purpose in my work, but the road I took to get here wasn't exactly a straight line. In fact, I embarked on several different career paths before I landed on the right one for me.

I probably took such a winding path to get here because I had such a difficult time growing up. School was never a place where I felt like I fit in. I struggled all the way through elementary school, especially when it came to reading. When a teacher would make me read out loud, I would stumble over my words and kids would laugh at me. People started to think of me as *the dumb kid*—and not just my classmates, but teachers, too. I was teased as a result, and that led to my getting into fights on a pretty regular basis. Pretty soon I was considered an all-around problem child.

That's probably why in sixth grade, my teacher wanted to hold me back. I had butted heads with this teacher all year long, and she just had no tolerance for me. My parents had to go to meeting after meeting about the subject while my anxiety level just rose higher and higher. I already felt like I was seen as different from everyone else—and not in a good way. I thought being held back would make things so much worse.

In the end, my parents wouldn't let them do it, and I graduated with the rest of my class. I was so relieved at the time, but I realize now that the damage had already been done. By then I had fully bought into the idea that I was simply dumber than everyone else.

I am dyslexic, but finding that out didn't help—not at first, anyway. Among the tests I was made to take was an IQ test, on which I scored quite high, but even that couldn't change my perception of myself. It was ingrained by then. Back then it wasn't all that common for educators to understand how to diagnose something like dyslexia, let alone how to work with someone who had it. I always thought of my dyslexia as this thing I had to hide about myself, so I spent much of my childhood trying to do just that. I spent so much energy on it, in fact, that by the time I graduated from high school, I didn't have a clue what I wanted or what I was good at. So I joined the Air Force. What else was I going to do?

I actually excelled in the Air Force, becoming part of an elite military police force responsible for transporting Priority A Resources. But then my career was abruptly cut short by a previously undiagnosed heart condition that forced me out of my unit. After that I ended up back in the States, where I got a job with a boat charter company because it was somewhere I could work part-time while going to college. I stayed with that company for more than ten years, and during that time, I mentored (or what I would now call "coached") a lot of young employees. But eventually I realized that working for a boat charter company wasn't what I wanted to do with the rest of my life.

After that, I went searching, educating myself about various options, trying out another career or two in the process. (How I eventually found my way to coaching top professional athletes is something I will talk more about in later chapters.) But what I was really searching for was myself: What did I value? What was my real purpose? What could I really contribute to this world?

One of my biggest self-coaching moments came during that period of my life when I started to question my own beliefs about who I was. In the back of my mind, I was still this dyslexic kid who had to work twice as hard as everyone else to fit in while also hiding what I saw as this painful

TAKE CHARGE OF YOU

flaw about myself. It gradually dawned on me that my "flaw" made me different in some really useful ways. For example, I had developed a heightened awareness of the people around me, how they functioned, how they thought, and what made them tick. I had initially developed these skills in order to protect myself from people who might judge or look down on me. But when I figured out that I didn't really need to protect myself anymore, I realized those same skills were things I could actually *offer* to people. I could use them to help others reach their full potential.

The way I thought about myself was flipped completely on its head. It turns out that the learning *disability* I had tried to hide for so long has actually given me unique *abilities*. And that reframing, that change in perspective, opened up a world of possibilities for me. (It's also a key self-coaching skill that we will teach you in this book.) It's what put me on the path to becoming a professional coach who gets to help

---

I remember something my dad had said to us—it seems like a hundred times. He would say: "We may not have the nicest car. You may not live in the nicest house. You may not wear the nicest clothes every day, but always remember, no one can beat you at being you." No one can beat you at being you. So whenever you feel as though you're not achieving the thing that you believe that you deserve, just focus on being the best you that you can be.

—MARVIN ELLISON, CEO of Lowe's

---

people become their best selves each and every day—and what could be better than that?

What It Really Means to Coach

Think about a plant you might have in the corner of your office or at home in your living room. You want that plant to thrive and grow tall, but often it won't do that without some help. Perhaps it's not getting enough light or water. Maybe there isn't enough space around it to stretch its roots. It might be exposed to less-than-optimal temperatures or poor-quality soil. Any number of things could be getting in its way.

Now, if you know something about this particular plant and are paying attention, you can help. Of course, it's not going to benefit the plant if you berate it for not being taller or take its branches in your hands and try to force them to stretch. But you can help in other ways—by moving it to a brighter spot, if that's what it needs, or repotting it in a larger container with more room to grow. You can't change the plant's basic nature, but with the right awareness and actions, you can work with what you have and create conditions that give it the best chance to thrive.

It's the same with self-coaching. You don't need to reject your fundamental nature or change who you are at your core to reach your full potential. You're not going to try to force growth, or to blame, shame, or berate it out of yourself.

What you need is to develop a good understanding of who you are and what drives you. And then you need a process, a kind of blueprint you can follow that will help you use that knowledge to create conditions that will allow you to grow and thrive. That's what this book offers you.

The temptation to lead as a chess master, controlling each move ... must give way to an approach as a gardener, enabling rather than directing. A gardening approach to leadership is anything but passive.

—GENERAL STANLEY MCCHRYSTAL, U.S. Army, retired[6]

Despite this book's title, you won't really be going it alone. We will use our combined years of experience to act as your surrogate coaches, providing the insight, information, and motivation you need to grow yourself personally and professionally. To that end, we have developed a simple, straightforward process that will guide you on your self-coaching journey. Step by step, it will help you hone in on what is really going to make a difference in your life, develop a specific action plan to make it real, and then provide the process and inspiration needed to see things through.

What's more, the book will unfold, not as a passive reading experience but as an interactive experience. Chock full of exercises, tips, and questions to ask yourself to spark insight, it's designed to provide not just the knowledge you need, but also the tools to turn that knowledge into real, lasting change.

Along the way, our guidance will be brought to life by inspiring stories from top performers in a wide range of fields. In addition to our own experiences, you will hear from people like legendary NFL quarterback Tom Brady; one of the world's longest-serving female CEOs, Indra Nooyi of PepsiCo; one of *Fortune*'s "World's Greatest Leaders," Marvin Ellison, CEO of Lowe's; one of *Fortune* magazine's "Most Powerful Women in Business," Lynne Doughtie of KPMG; star of the Bravo TV shows *Million Dollar Listing* and *Sell It Like Serhant*, Ryan Serhant; superstar southern chef Edward Lee; commissioner of the WNBA and the first female CEO of Deloitte, Cathy Englebert; financial industry giants like JPMorgan Chase CEO Jamie Dimon; tech industry leaders like Tony Xu of DoorDash; some of the world's top athletes, past and present, like Justin Rose, Jason Day, Larry Fitzgerald, Meghan Klingenberg, and Raymond Floyd; and many more.

With all that wisdom collected in one place, paired with an easy to follow, step by step process and exercises designed to spur real transformation, we believe you can't help but succeed if you give self-coaching a chance. No more waiting for the right coach to come along. Or, even if you have a coach or mentor, no more relying on that person's insights alone. It's time to take your personal growth and professional development into your own hands.

The only thing you need to get started is a desire to access more of your potential and a willingness to keep an open mind. After that, you can coach yourself wherever you want to go.

Take Charge Action: Get Ready to Coach Yourself

This book is meant to be more than just something you read and then put back on the shelf. It's meant to be something you use, a blueprint to take you from where you are now to where you want to go. To that end, you will find what we call Take Charge Actions throughout this book: exercises and tools that will help you practice the skills you need to consistently move yourself forward.

That *practice* is a crucial part of any person's growth and success, so we hope you will take it seriously and spend time on it rather than rushing through this book. For his podcast, "How Leaders Lead with David Novak," David once interviewed Cathy Englebert. Before her leadership roles at the WNBA and Deloitte, she was an athlete at Lehigh University, where she played basketball for Hall of Fame coach Muffet McGraw. Englebert still remembers how McGraw always used to tell the team, "The game is won in practice, so practice as hard as you play in the game." Englebert took that lesson with her when she went into the business world. "The game is not won when one thing is on the line," she explained. "It's won in all the *preparation* leading up to closing a big deal or driving a big new revenue stream."

With that idea in mind, we encourage you to prepare yourself now to make the most out of the Take Charge Actions we provide you. Depending on what works best for you, you might want to get a notebook dedicated to working through this process—a place where you can write down the answers to questions, do the exercises, and make note of your progress. Or, if you prefer, you can go to **takechargeofyou.com**, where we have a digital option that you can use for the same purpose.

That's your very first assignment: Whichever method works best for you, prepare yourself now to put in the practice time. And then, whenever you see the 🔋 icon throughout this book, use it as a cue that it's time to get practicing!

The Self-Coaching Conversation

Ask Yourself Some Key Questions

• • • • • • • •

Your Self-Coaching Conversation Toolkit

 Find Your Joy Blockers

 Find Your Joy Builders

 Discover Your Single Biggest Thing

 Envision Your Destination

TIP KEY

TAKE CHARGE

SELF-COACHING

It is not the answer that enlightens, but the question.

—EUGÈNE IONESCO, playwright[7]

If you have found your way to this book, it probably means that you are searching for something. Perhaps you are not fully satisfied with how things are going in your career or your life. Maybe there's a goal you'd like to reach or an issue you'd like to resolve, but you're not quite sure how to get there. Or maybe you're really pretty happy, but still looking for new ways to grow and succeed, to continually up your game.

It's situations like these where a good coach can really come in handy—to help you gain perspective, develop a plan, work through the inevitable hurdles, and provide inspiration and motivation to see things through. So that the growth and change you're looking for can become more than just a hope or desire. So that it can take shape and become reality.

If you're going to coach yourself through all that, where do you start?

When either of us set out to coach someone new, we always start in the same place: with a conversation. You have to get to know a bit about the person you're coaching—about who they are, what they want, what they believe is getting in their way—before you can begin to offer any useful guidance.

With that in mind, we are going to spend this chapter guiding you through a kind of conversation with yourself. We do this so we can begin to do two important things that will be key on your self-coaching journey:

1) Gain a better understanding of how best to coach the unique individual that is you.

2) Figure out what we will be coaching you toward.

Right about now you may be thinking, "I don't need to do that. I already know enough about myself and what I want, so let's just get moving already!" We know the feeling, but let us explain why skipping this step or rushing through it may not be the best idea.

The first thing we will guide you to do—gain a better understanding of how best to coach the unique individual that is you—comes from our combined experience as professionals who have coached a wide range of people and personalities. Through these experiences we have learned an important lesson: What works for one person doesn't always work for the next. This means that while we can give you a process to follow, it's not going to work unless, along the way, you take into account who *you* are and what *you* want, which isn't always as easy as it sounds.

For his podcast, David interviewed Tom Brady, seven-time Super Bowl champion and quarterback for the Tampa Bay Buccaneers, who had a simple example of this. Back when he was with the New England Patriots, Brady discovered that a lot of his teammates, especially the younger ones, looked to him for encouragement. They wanted a shout-out when they did something right, and when they got it, it motivated them to try even harder. But wide receiver Julian Edelman was different. He didn't want shout-outs. In fact, Edelman got downright uncomfortable whenever Brady told him he had done a good job. "If you say something nice, he doesn't even know what to do," Brady explained. Brady learned that challenging Edelman to do better was far more motivating for him than paying him a compliment. A simple shift in the way Brady communicated made all the difference, but it came as a result of something that wasn't so simple: gaining an understanding of where Edelman was coming from and appreciating that uniqueness. It also helped him realize that he needed to find out what moti-vated each of his team members in order to get the best out of them because the same approach wasn't going to work for everyone. That same insight applies to you—you have to know yourself in order to know how best to coach yourself to success.

The second thing we will help you do—figure out what we will be coaching you toward—is a practical neces-sity. After all, coaching should not be an aimless pursuit. In fact, if you don't have a clear idea of your destination, you can easily waste a lot of time and resources only to go nowhere—or nowhere good. Jason learned this lesson the hard way before he became a coach. Back then, he was working as director of operations for a boat charter company in San Diego, and it was a good job. He made good money, received excellent benefits, and he really liked his boss. A lot of people would say that he was in an enviable position. The problem was that after twelve years with the company, Jason felt like he had outgrown his position, and there was nowhere to go. The only person above him was his boss, and Jason didn't want his boss's job. Jason spent his days outdoors, on the boats, interacting with customers and employees. In contrast, his boss could usually be found in his office, sitting behind a desk, interacting with files and a computer screen. Jason couldn't imagine that for himself.

Jason found himself in a situation practically everyone will encounter at some point in their careers: He was no longer feeling inspired by his work, his motivation had waned as a result, and he was left feeling stuck, unsure what to do about any of it. It felt like perhaps it was time to try something new, but there was also a lot of fear and anxiety around whether that was the right choice and whether he would be able to find something better. After all, it had been a great place to work for a number of years, and his boss had been an important mentor to him. Under his guidance, Jason had gotten the chance to start developing his managerial and coaching skills, which are so important to the work he does today as a performance coach. It was a lot to leave behind, but after months of agonizing about it, he decided there was not much he could do but resign.

He and his wife, Elizabeth, then decided to try real estate development. They would buy a house, fix it up, sell it for a profit, and then repeat the process all over again. They were successful enough at it that they were able to sell their home in San Diego and move to Palm Springs, where Jason could better pursue one of his life's biggest passions: golf.

The two moved into a house on the grounds of PGA West, home of the Bob Hope Classic, where Jason became a member. All of a sudden he went from squeezing in a few rounds on a public course before work to having access to nine courses at one of the country's most prestigious private clubs. Thanks to the nature of his real estate work, his schedule was flexible enough that he could play anytime he wanted. He even had his own golf cart in the garage. Having grown up without a lot of money, being part of an exclusive country club with all the attendant perks was nothing short of amazing. It was what he always thought he wanted. Finally, he was living the dream.

Only it didn't feel like a dream. The move, the change of careers, the change in lifestyle, it was all supposed to make Jason happier and more fulfilled, but it had the opposite effect. Jason found himself more miserable than he had ever been in his life, and he wasn't sure why.

If you think about it, it can be quite easy to make big moves in your life or career. Something as potentially life changing as quitting a job takes nothing more than a conversation with your boss or a dashed-off email of resignation. Making *the right* big moves, however, takes more time, thought, and planning. It also requires a good amount of self-knowledge in order to know what *right* means for you, so that's where we begin—by simply listening to ourselves just like any good coach would when meeting us for the first time.

This chapter will guide you through a series of key questions to ask yourself in order to kick off your self-coaching journey on the right foot. Once again, these questions will help you do two things:

1) Gain a better understanding of how best to coach the unique individual that is you.

2) Figure out what we will be coaching you toward.

SELF-COACHING TIP: When asking yourself the questions in this chapter, there's no need to judge your answers. Don't worry about what the answers mean or whether they will lead you toward something that feels impossible to achieve. We have plenty of time in the coming chapters to convert the answers into action, even to tweak or change them if necessary. Right now we're in discovery mode. We're brainstorming and collecting information. We're focused on simply asking questions and listening to the thoughts they provoke in order to find out what we can learn about ourselves that will be useful in our self-coaching journey.

Key Question #1: What's Getting in the Way of Your Joy?

When Jason realized the career transition he had made wasn't right for him, it was really nothing more than a feeling that clued him in. He felt miserable, and that misery prompted him to ask himself why.

There were a number of reasons why, but one of the big reasons was that, when Jason left behind the boat charter company, he didn't realize he was also leaving behind a key part of his work that had brought him real joy. He had always loved working with people and feeling like he was making a difference in their lives, something he had ample opportunity to do there because it was a business where young and part-time workers were constantly cycling in and out as summer help or side jobs while they went to college. He got a chance to mentor so many of those people the same way his boss had mentored him. But fixing up houses? That was largely a solitary pursuit. Working on his own didn't feel purposeful to him.

That didn't mean that it was the wrong decision to leave his job at the boat company. It just meant that the next step he chose on his career path wasn't exactly right for him, either. Back then he wasn't asking himself these kinds of questions, but you can begin to see how, once he started to, he found his way to becoming a performance coach, a career where he gets to work with people and make a difference in their lives each and every day—something that feels much more joyful and purposeful to him.

Many of us are in the habit of ignoring or pushing past our feelings, especially when they're unhappy ones like misery, or even simply feeling stuck or uninspired. But we can also look at feelings as simply a source of information about ourselves. They can help us gain insight into what's going wrong or what's going right in our lives, whether we're on the right track or headed in the wrong direction, whether we need to make a change and what that change might be.

With that in mind, we're going to start by focusing on one particular feeling: *joy*—or the case of this first question, the lack of it. (The next question will focus on what will bring you more of it.) Why start with joy? It may sound like an impractical or unsubstantial word, but think about the difference between doing something because you *have to* and doing something because you *want to*—because you love it and it makes you feel happy or joyful to do it. Those *have tos* are the things we often complain about, rush through, get to only after a lot of procrastination, or avoid altogether when possible. The *want tos* are the things we willingly make time for, can't wait to do, and put our best efforts toward because we enjoy them so much. In terms of an organizing principle for continual growth and development, which do you think will lead you to be more successful: pursuing joy when and wherever possible, or doing what you feel like you should or have to?

Of course no one is perfectly joyful all the time. Even the things that make us feel joy can take hard work and even sacrifice to attain. So no, we're not inviting you to skip your dentist appointment or eat cheeseburgers for breakfast, lunch, and dinner just because it makes you feel joyful in the moment. (After all, any joy you get from these things could easily be undercut later on due to unwanted consequences!) What we're going to do here, over the next few sections, is use joy as your *destination finder*. When you get into your car and set out on a journey to someplace new, the first thing you typically do is type your destination into the GPS. That's how you decide which route is best to take to get to where you want to go. This is something we have all done countless times before. But let's back up for a moment. In order to do that, first you have to know what your destination should be. How do you decide where you want to go in the first place?

When you choose a destination in this self-coaching process, you are choosing a direction for where you want to take your life or career in the future. Once you do that, the work becomes about planning your route, making steady progress, dealing with the inevitable potholes or roadblocks along the way, and maybe even making changes on the fly if circumstances change. All that can translate into a lot of work, so before expending all that energy, let's spend some time making sure—to the best of our abilities in this moment—that we're choosing a destination that's worth our efforts. Joy is the tool we're going to use to help us do that, and we start with what in our lives is getting in the way of it.

TAKE CHARGE ACTION:
Find Your Joy Blockers

We are going to start in a simple, straightforward way, by asking you to make a list. You don't need to over-think this task. There are no right or wrong answers. Just find a quiet time and place to do this exercise, follow the steps, and accept what comes up as information you can use on your journey.

1) Ask yourself the question: "What's getting in the way of my joy?" You may even want to ask it out loud to yourself.

2) Sit with the question for a moment.

3) Write down whatever comes to mind.

ADDITIONAL TACTICS TO TRY: There are different ways to approach or think through any question. If you're having trouble answering the question or if nothing much comes immediately to mind, try the following tactics.

- Think back to some of your worst days—those days when you have felt the most frustrated, unhappy, or unfulfilled. What was happening that made those days so difficult for you? What about those days made you feel less than joyful?
- If it's helpful to spur or organize your thinking, try dividing the page into categories—work, home life, personal relationships, spiritual/community life, personal growth, and anything else that resonates with you. Then ask yourself the question as it applies to each category. For example:

  - What's getting in the way of my joy *at work*?
  - What's getting in the way of my joy *at home*?
  - What's getting in the way of my joy *in my personal relationships*?

- Once you have something on the page, read it back and ask yourself, "Could my answer be more specific?" For example, perhaps you wrote down: "My job is getting in the way of my joy." That's a pretty broad response, so try digging a little deeper. What about your job makes you feel that way? Is there a key part of it that you really dislike? Is it that you don't feel like your contribution is appreciated? Is it that you dislike your boss or your coworkers? Is it that you'd rather be in a different role or industry? Are the hours such that you come home too late to see your kids before they go to sleep? Is the commute killing you? You see what we mean. There are so many reasons why you might not like the work you do, so try to zero in on the specific causes.

When you answer this question, maybe just a few key things come to mind. Maybe you end up with a whole long list of things that are drowning out your joy. Maybe you even draw a blank. Whatever the case, that's okay. Give it your best effort, write down whatever comes to mind, and keep going. You can always come back to this exercise later and add to your list or try again. Remember, we're simply brainstorming here, collecting information, so the fact that you might struggle to answer the question is information in itself that we can use going forward.

Key Question #2: What Would Grow Your Joy Personally or Professionally?

Self-coaching is about growth and positive change. It's about setting your sights on a destination that's going to make a difference in your life and finding the will and ability to get there. This question is the next step on the path to figuring out where to focus your sights, and it's simply a reversal of the first. Instead of what's getting in the way of your joy, we're now asking you to look at what would bring you more of it.

You probably have a natural sense of what joy means to you, at least enough to begin to answer that last question about what could be blocking it. It's good to have tuned into your natural instincts about it, but let's take a moment now to look more closely at the definition of joy in case it further informs your answer to these questions. Researchers who study joy (yes, there are people with that joyful job) generally define it as an intense positive feeling. Ingrid Fetell Lee, author of *Joyful*, is one of those who made a thorough study of the subject, and she proposed that "while contentment is curled up on the sofa, and bliss is lost in tranquil meditation, joy is skipping, jiving, twirling, giggling."

"It is a uniquely exuberant emotion," Fetell Lee continued, "a high-energy form of happiness."[8]

That "high-energy" part is important. People who love what they do often say they feel energized by it. People who don't feel the opposite.

David learned this lesson early, when he was still in college. He was enrolled in the journalism school at the University of Missouri, and he was an okay student even though during his first couple years he probably spent as much time with his fraternity brothers as he did with his coursework. But then he took his first class in advertising and everything changed. He was no longer just going through the motions of doing what was expected of him to get a degree. He loved what he was learning so much, he couldn't get enough. He took more and more advertising and marketing classes, and along the way he went from making mostly Cs in his first two years to nearly all As. He was even named Outstanding Male Student in Advertising his senior year (much to the dismay of those fraternity brothers he used to spend so much time with). Even better, he had found a career path he couldn't wait to pursue.

He was lucky to learn that lesson early because it really informed his entire career. Looking back now, he sees most of his big decisions as based in joy. He realized early that when he cared about a subject, he wanted to learn as much as he could about it. He also realized that when he learned something important, he loved sharing it with others. That's why, when he was at Yum! Brands, he gathered all the insights he had gained over the years and put together a program to teach people how to become better leaders. He called the program Taking People with You, and as CEO, he personally taught it to more than 4,000 people. Nothing wore him out more because he felt compelled to put the whole of his energy into it, but nothing left him feeling more satisfied either. The program was such a success that he was driven to share it with even more people, which is why he wrote a book of the same name. Watching it become a bestseller brought him so much joy that he was driven to write more books after that, including this one. It's also why he started his podcast, so he could bring the insights of so many great leaders to people who might not otherwise get a chance to learn from them.

Joy has an energy to it, one that can snowball, leading to more and more things you find yourself driven to do. So as you answer the next question, keep this definition of joy in mind. It's not just about what makes you happy, but what makes you feel energized and alive.

TAKE CHARGE ACTION:
Find Your Joy Builders

Once again, find a quiet time and place for this exercise.

1) Start by thinking about what would grow your joy. Take some time to really imagine this.

2) Look back at your answers to the previous question and try flipping them on their heads. For example, if you said your contentious relationship with your office mate is getting in the way of your joy at work, would transferring to a different department or company bring you joy? Would finding a way to improve the relationship do it? (Remember, we're not worried about *how* to make this happen just yet, only *what* we want to happen.)

3) Consider anything else that would bring more joy into your life. For example, perhaps you get a lot of joy out of the volunteer work you do

twice a month working with kids at your local community center. Would it bring you more joy to do it more often, maybe even full-time?

4) Write down as many Joy Builders as you can think of. Don't question what comes to mind. Just record it.

ADDITIONAL TACTICS TO TRY: If this question feels too broad or if you're finding it difficult to answer, try the following:

- Once again, you can break down the question into categories if it helps you: What brings you joy *at work*? What brings you joy *in your personal relationships*? And so on. (See the previous exercise for more suggested categories.)
- Try thinking about some of the best, most memorable days you have ever had—days when you felt your most purposeful, most powerful, and most joyful. What was happening that made that time stand out?

Sometimes people just come to work saying, "Hey, it's a job." It's not a job. It's a calling. It's a passion. It's something that consumes your life. And you've got to come in with a sense of optimism. You've got to come in with the sense of "I can do it." A sense of "I can do it; it must be done. I'm going to get everybody with me to get it done." There's got to be this constant love for [what you do].

—**INDRA NOOYI,** former chairman and CEO of PepsiCo

Key Question #3: What's the Single Biggest Thing You Can Imagine That Would Grow Your Joy Personally or Professionally?

The first two key questions were about starting to gain a better understanding of the *you* you will be coaching in this book. This question is about choosing a destination that we will be coaching you toward. To answer it, you are going to use the work you have done so far examining your Joy Blockers and Joy Builders. And then, when considering all those joy related things, this question becomes about focus and selection: Which *one* thing will bring you the *most* joy— that's your Single Biggest Thing (SBT). That's the destination we will coach you toward through the course of this book.

Early in his career, David realized that he hated the feeling of getting stuck. He always felt driven to learn new things, expand his experience and capabilities, and take on new challenges. It sucked the joy out of his work when he didn't feel this way.

He felt his joy being blocked when he was working at an ad agency as the management supervisor for the agency's biggest and most important client, Frito-Lay. At the time, the company had hired a new executive creative director from a Chicago ad agency. In the past, she had come up with some iconic campaigns, so she was tasked with developing a campaign for Frito-Lay. She came up with something she loved, but David hated it. He had been working with Frito-Lay for a while, and he believed it was the wrong approach for the client.

David went to his boss, who was the head of the agency, with his concerns, but he was told he had to support her. What's more, he had to get behind the agency point of view and go with her to pitch the campaign to the client. It felt deflating to try to sell something he didn't believe in. And in the end, his instincts were right. The executives at Frito-Lay couldn't believe he would bring them something that was so far away from what they wanted.

That wasn't David's only clue about what he wanted. He would also develop operating plans for the agency's clients, which would so often get sold to clients who wouldn't execute them well—or sometimes at all. They were just recommendations after all, and the client could take them or leave them. It was frustrating for him to cede control in situations like these. It made him feel stuck, like he wasn't getting to see his vision through or find out if his ideas would work or not.

Paying attention to how he felt in these moments is what led David to decide that his SBT, the thing he wanted most, was to run something someday—to be the one in charge of his own division or company so he wouldn't be constrained by these kinds of limitations. He wanted a chance to test himself and find out what he was capable of. It was a big idea, a far-away destination, and it was always in the back of his mind.

That is a crucial part of choosing your SBT: It should feel big, important, impactful, even aspirational. There is a difference between setting a goal and choosing a destination. A goal might be to lose five pounds or get into the habit of exercising five times a week. The destination might be to improve your overall health to the point where you have more energy, more focus, and you feel like you're living your best life. So allow yourself to think big, think boldly, and see where it takes you.

TAKE CHARGE ACTION:
Discover Your Single Biggest Thing

1) Return to the list of Joy Builders that you made and read through them. Put a check mark next to the ones that feel the biggest and most important.

2) If you could pick only one thing to focus on, what would it be? Ask yourself: What would make the biggest difference if I started working toward it today?

3) This is your Single Biggest Thing—the destination you're going to work toward throughout the rest of this book. Write it down and draw a circle around it.

ADDITIONAL TACTICS TO TRY: The following are some hints to get your juices flowing if you're having trouble.

- Look for commonalities in your Joy Blocker and Joy Builder lists, and ask yourself whether they can be combined into a larger vision or destination. For example, maybe you said it blocks your joy when your boss tells you that you can't pursue a new idea or innovation that you're excited about. Maybe you also said you feel most joyful at work when you're running a project on your own. Maybe you remembered a time in your life when you were self-employed and how much joy you got from the sense of freedom and control. If you look at these things together, might they suggest that the larger thing you really want is to start your own business? Or, like David, you want to run your own division or organization one day?

- David was recently talking with an acquaintance who had lost someone close to him, and the experience really gave the person focus. He wasn't in a career that he loved, and he realized he didn't want to waste another day *not* pursuing his passion. We can all take a lesson from that. You don't have to wait until tragedy strikes to ask yourself what you might regret if it did. One way to approach the question of finding your SBT is this: At the end of your life, what would you look back and regret not trying to achieve?

SELF-COACHING TIP: You may have noticed that the previous question asked what would most grow joy *personally or professionally.* As far as we're concerned, the process is the same whether you use this book to coach yourself toward a personal destination, a professional destination, or both. So try to keep an open mind about what might truly make the biggest difference for you in any part of your life.

EXAMPLES OF SBTS: PERSONAL, PROFESSIONAL, OR BOTH

- Start my own business and become my own boss.
- Take charge of my health and well-being by getting into the best shape possible.
- Find out if I can make it as a professional coach, athlete, singer, actor, or [fill in the blank].
- Go back to school and get my doctoral degree.
- Create a podcast that people actually listen to and gets out my message.
- Become the head of my division or company.
- Get my real estate license without sacrificing the work-life balance that's so important to me; in other words, continuing be the best parent I can be.
- Finish writing my novel or screenplay.
- Finally make that big move to a new town and to the new home I've been dreaming about.
- Figure out what my next act will be when I change careers or retire.

What to Do When Doubt Creeps In

We mentioned how David had a destination in the back of his mind that he wanted to run something someday. Well, even further in the back of his mind were gnawing doubts that would sometimes break through and make him wonder whether that goal was even possible for him. He had a bachelor's degree in journalism, but that's where his formal education ended. As he continued along his career path, it became clear that he was working alongside, and competing against, scores of people with MBA degrees. For a long time, he would excuse himself to go to the bathroom every time a conversation with a group of colleagues turned to where they went to graduate school, so he wouldn't have to admit that he didn't have an advanced degree.

There are always going to be reasons to not do something, why our minds tell us our SBT might just be too big or too impossible. Often when we think about making big changes in our lives or setting our sights on far-away destinations, the buts, what ifs, and naysaying thoughts ride in on the same wave. Let's acknowledge that fact and then actively choose to set them aside for just a little while. We're not going to ignore them, just deal with them in time. Because first things first: We want to get clear about what you really want *before* we address all the things that could potentially get in the way of it.

We say this now because these are the kind of thoughts that can drive you off course before you even get started.

Imagine if David had given in to those voices telling him he didn't have the credentials to pursue what he wanted? He never would have gone on to become president and then CEO of a Fortune 500 company, who later started his own business. So, as much as possible, allow yourself to think big, have courage, and keep your focus on your joy.

 SELF-COACHING TIP: If nagging doubts arise that threaten to derail your process—thoughts like *I really want that but it's impossible*—return to your list of Joy Blockers and add them to the list. Once you have done that, leave them there on the page and return to where you left off in this process. Writing something down can take away some of its power, and turning the page can signal to the part of your brain that has these concerns that, while you're not ignoring them, you're setting them aside to be addressed at another time.

What to Do If Your Answer to One or All of The Key Questions Is "I Don't Know"

We have talked about the fact that there was a point in Jason's experience when he didn't know the answer to the questions "What's getting in the way of my joy?" and "What would bring me more joy?" He knew he was unhappy in his new life and career, but he didn't know exactly why for some time. And the SBT that would have made a difference in his life? Well, that was a question mark too—until it wasn't.

If "I don't know" is what comes up for you right now for one or more of these questions, that doesn't mean your self-coaching journey has to come to an end. In fact, "I don't know" is a good indication that you need coaching now more than ever.

At this early stage, some people's SBTs are going to be very specific. Other people will find it challenging to figure out just what they want or need at a given moment. Destinations, like lives, are subject to change, so over the course of your life you are likely to find yourself in both these situations at different times.

One thing you can do to spur your thinking is to move the question outside of yourself. Often it's easier to analyze what's working and not working in other people's lives than it is to analyze our own. Think about whom you admire in different areas of your life. If you feel unsettled in your career, for example, think about whose career path you admire and ask yourself: "What does that person have that I don't have?" Then, "Is that something that might bring me joy too?"

Also remember what we said in the introduction to this book: self-coaching does not mean that you have to go it alone. If you have a friend, parent, spouse, or mentor whom you trust enough to ask for advice on this subject, then ask. Tell the person you are feeling stuck, uninspired, unhappy, or whatever describes your situation, and you are wondering what you could do to make a real difference in your life. Ask where in your life the person sees you expressing more joy and where you seem to show less of it. A word of caution, however: We will continue to talk throughout this book about getting help and counsel from the people around you, but at this early stage make sure to *only* ask people you know have your best interests at heart. And even then, don't take anything anyone else says as "the right answer." This is your life and your decisions, so consider anything you hear from others as simply more information, more fodder for your brainstorming, which you can choose to use or ignore as you see fit.

If none of this brings up much for you and you continue to be unsure about where you should be headed next, you can still work these steps. The SBT you set for yourself can be "to gain enough insight and self-awareness to answer these questions with more than an 'I don't know.'" That can be a big and important thing to do, so don't underestimate it as a potential destination that would make a real difference in your life right now. After all, what would it mean to you to be able to answer questions like these about yourself and your future with confidence and excitement? What would it mean to you to know you had a plan to bring more joy into your life? Might that be a big thing worth working toward?

Another idea to keep in mind: Don't underestimate the value of simply jumping in and trying something to see how it feels and gain some insight. Maybe you're in sales and you just know it's the wrong role for you, but the right role is unclear. You have been wondering if you might like marketing more, but you're unsure. Ask your boss if you can work on a project with the marketing department in your spare time. See how it feels, and along the way keep asking yourself, "Does this bring me joy?"

As David likes to say, sometimes you hit the bull's eye because you just know in your gut what you want. But other times it may feel like you're flying in circles around your destination, trying to pinpoint its location. That's okay. You can keep flying in tighter and tighter circles until you hone in on your SBT. And along the way, let joy be your guide.

Key Question #4: What Would It Mean If You Accomplished Your Single Biggest Thing?

When describing how he feels about his work, world-renowned investor Warren Buffett likes to say it's like he "tap dances to work" every day. This is something David was lucky enough to witness for himself when, as the new head of Yum! Brands, he would visit Buffett annually to learn more about the finance side of running a company. They would meet each year at a KFC, and Buffett would always ask a million questions. He always wanted to go behind the scenes to see the operation and meet everyone who worked there—all of whom he had questions for as well. He had this infectious desire to learn and to get better at what he did. David got a lot out of those meetings, not the least of which was how important it was to love what you do and to show that each and every day.

Buffett has mentioned that image of himself tap dancing to work so often that his biographer, Carol Loomis, used it as the title for her book about him. It's very appealing. Who wouldn't want to feel that way when they walk into work every morning? How much better would life be if you did?

We want to end this chapter by asking you to create a picture of your own, one that describes what it would be like to achieve what you want most in your life.

TAKE CHARGE ACTION:
Envision Your Destination

1) Look back at the Single Biggest Thing you wrote down. Do this even if you have the kind of placeholder SBT that we just talked about. (It might be something like: "Gain more insight into what I want so I can answer these questions" or "Try something new so I can decide whether it can be my next SBT.")

2) Instead of thinking about how you're going to accomplish your goal, start with the end result in mind. Imagine what it would be like to have *already* reached your destination and accomplished your SBT.

3) Describe what that would be like. What would it feel like? How might your life change? What might it mean to you personally? What might it mean to your family, friends, or community?

4) Take some time with this and write down as much as you can think of. Once you have finished, read it back to yourself. You will want to remember the feelings that come up because they can serve as powerful motivators throughout this process as you encounter the inevitable roadblocks and do the hard work of achieving your SBT.

5) To help you stay motivated through this process, sum up your key thoughts and feelings in just a few words—it might be something like "I get to leave the house every morning feeling like I'm tap dancing to work." Write them on a sticky note along with your SBT. Then post the note on your bathroom mirror, next to your computer monitor, on the home screen of your phone, or someplace where you will see it regularly so it can serve as a reminder, a focus, and an inspiration moving forward.

ADDITIONAL TACTICS TO TRY:

- We want you to really exercise your imagination muscles here and spend some time picturing the difference your SBT could make in your life. If you're a visual person, try drawing what it would feel like to accomplish your SBT rather than (or in addition to) writing about it. Or make a collage of images; people have been using vision boards or mood boards in this way for years. (Google the terms if you want inspiration; you'll find countless examples.) If that's what works for you, then do it!
- To spur your thinking even further, try imagining your destination using each of your five senses. When you have realized your SBT

  ... what might it *look* like?

  ... what might it *sound* like?

  ... what might it *smell* like?

  ... what might it *taste* like?

  ... what might it *feel* like?

This may seem like an odd approach, but everyone's brain works differently and different senses spark more for some of us than for others. For example, Jason used to coach a minor league pitcher who said he could just *hear* when a pitch was thrown well. The whoosh of the ball moving through the air in a particular way was etched into his brain. A good fastball sounded one way, a curveball another, a slider yet another, and a botched pitch, well that sounded entirely different. Past coaches had told this pitcher that relying on his hearing was ridiculous at his level, but Jason disagreed. If it worked for him to imagine the sound of a pitch before he threw it, then why wouldn't he continue doing what worked?

Give it a try. If it's a promotion you're looking for, perhaps the sound of someone calling you by your new title is what comes to mind. Or, you might visualize what your new office will look like and what you will do in there. You might even imagine what it would smell like (the scent of a new leather chair, perhaps?), if that's what gets your mind going.

By now you have started to gain a better understanding of the *you* you will be coaching through the rest of this book and the destination you will be coaching yourself toward.

We're going to continue to work with your answers to these key questions throughout this process so keep them handy. We will return to them, consider them from different angles, bring more insight to them, and maybe even adjust or change them. Coaching yourself is a process, and we have just begun. We're going to continue your journey in the next chapter by looking at, and practicing, the kind of mindset that will best enable you to coach yourself to do big things.

If you're going to be successful, you have to figure out what it takes to motivate you, drive you, and well, just get you to be the best that you can be.

—JUNIOR BRIDGEMAN, owner and CEO, Heartland Coca-Cola Bottling Co.

2

The Self-Coaching Mindset

Open Yourself Up to Growth

• • • • • • • •

Your Self-Coaching Mindset Toolkit

 Change Your *Nots* into *Not Yets*

 Practice Detachment Breathing

 Put Yourself in a Neutral State

 Shift Your Focus

 Balance Your Negatives with Positives

 Prioritize What You Value Most

 Define Your Purpose

Mindset change is not about picking up a few pointers here and there. It's about seeing things in a new way.

—CAROL DWECK, professor of psychology at Stanford University[9]

In this chapter, you're going to set aside the answers to the questions we just talked about, only for a little while. This may feel counterintuitive, even frustrating. After all, many of us are action-oriented people. If something is wrong, we want to fix it. If we have a destination in mind, we want to start moving toward it. *Not* acting can feel like the wrong thing when we know there's something we want to accomplish.

But this is exactly where we're going to start this chapter and for good reason. There's a popular quote that Jason likes to tell his clients: "You can't solve a problem from the same mind that created it." If you want to solve a problem in your life or career, if you want to change something, if you want to do something new, you first need to work toward a new way of thinking.

The concepts we're going to talk you through here will help you adopt a new way of thinking that we call the *coaching mindset.* So what does that mean? A coaching mindset is when your mind is open to whatever is going to drive your growth or performance. That means avoiding the trap of preconceived notions or prejudging what's going to happen. Instead, you want to be continually searching for the next insight that's going to move you forward and closer to your destination.

Too often people think of a coach as the person with all the answers, but a good coach is really more of a seeker. This is true whether you are coaching someone else or you are coaching yourself. Seeking knowledge to better understand the people you coach (even when it's you) and the things that impact them is how coaches come up with new ideas, insights, and innovations that can help.

David learned a lot about this approach from the late, great John Wooden, head basketball coach at UCLA, who led his team to win ten NCAA national championships in just twelve years. You might think that someone with such a stellar track record had more than enough knowledge and insight to coach any player well, but that never stopped Wooden from believing he could always gain more. He is often quoted as saying, "It's what you learn after you know it all that counts." For example, when a player named Lew Alcindor (later known as Kareem Abdul-Jabbar) joined his team, it was the first time Wooden had ever coached someone so tall. Of course basketball players are known for their height, but at seven-foot-one, Alcindor was what Wooden respectfully described as an "extra tall player." He decided he needed to learn everything he could about how best to coach someone like that, so he did his homework. He talked with Wilt Chamberlain (also seven-foot-one), who played in the NBA at the time. He contacted other coaches who had worked with extra tall players. And he must have done something right because Alcindor went on to have a record-breaking run at UCLA, with eighty-eight wins and just two losses during his three seasons with the team.[10]

In many ways, what you're trying to do as a coach is to keep your mind open enough to continue that conversation we started in the last chapter. You want to be flexible in your thinking and ready to explore, rather than believing you already have the answers to how you're going to accomplish your Single Biggest Thing—or even if it's possible. When Jason first decided he wanted to be a golf coach, he had a professional background that consisted of real estate, boat charters, and the military—but no golf. He'd never played professionally or even in college, so he had this recurring worry that no one in the golf world would trust him enough to hire him. If he had taken that thought at face value, it would have been the end of the conversation and there would have been nothing left to explore. But he kept his mind open and found his way to a whole new career. The same could have been true for David if he had given in to his concerns that not having an MBA would hold him back from becoming a leader in a top company. He never got an MBA, but he became CEO of a Fortune 500 company all the same.

When you can keep an open mind and look at a situation in terms of its possibilities instead of its potential limitations, it invites more questions and the conversation can continue. *If this is what I want to accomplish, then what do I need to do to*:

- *Build the necessary skills?*
- *Gain the right experience?*
- *Find relevant opportunities?*
- *Convince people of my value?*
- *Support myself and my family while I explore my options?*

When we set out to achieve something, especially something big, there are a lot of things that can get in the way or send us off course. Our own minds may be the biggest culprit. That's why adopting a coaching mindset early in this process is crucial to your success going forward. It's so important that we're going to work on building and practicing it now, before we apply it to your SBT.

In this chapter, we will talk about four key aspects of a coaching mindset. To be a good coach, you have to know how to draw on your capacity for:

1) Belief
2) Neutrality
3) Awareness
4) Self-knowledge

THE COACHING MINDSET: A DEFINITION
Your mind is open to whatever is going to drive your growth or performance, which means avoiding the trap of preconceived notions or prejudging what's going to happen. Instead, you are continually searching for the next insight that's going to move you forward.

The Action of Belief

Think back to the first coach you ever had in your life. For most of us, it was the coach of some youth sport or activity, like little league baseball, soccer, gymnastics, tennis, swimming, cheerleading, debate team, or something else. If you've never had a coach, think about a parent, teacher, or older sibling who taught you to do something you had never done before. Can you still remember the first time someone handed you something like a racket or a ball or a pencil and showed you what to do with it? Even if you can't, it probably won't stretch your imagination to think that whoever that person was, he or she did so *believing* that you could learn how to do it even though you had never done it before. Otherwise why bother?

Any new destination you set out to reach, anything new you set out to try, comes with unknowns. How do I know I have what it takes? How do I figure out what I need to do?

How do I know others will support my vision? The truth is that you don't know any of these things, not for sure. What's more, you will never know until you try, which is what makes it an act of belief, or even of faith, to attempt something you have never done before. Before you can accomplish anything, you have to be like your first little league coach, or whoever it was, and believe you have a chance of succeeding before you even try.

Just as important is belief because of how it changes the way you view and approach challenges. No path to accomplishing an SBT is going to be free of challenges, but whether you meet them or are thrown off course by them depends in large part on your capacity to believe. As prolific author and psychology professor Wayne Dyer once put it, "if you believe it will work out, you'll see opportunities. If you believe it won't, you will see obstacles." How we frame a situation in our minds can make an enormous difference.

Of course belief is a tricky thing—and sometimes a shaky thing. It may be there one moment and gone the next. But that doesn't mean you have no control over it. There are things all of us can do to cultivate our belief in ourselves and what we want to accomplish.

One thing we can do is learn to *reframe* the voices in our heads that undermine our belief. Those are the ones that tell us we can't, we shouldn't, or that we're not good enough— the ones that say it's not going to work out or it's too scary to even try. Reframing is a psychological technique that asks us to identify how we view a situation or experience and then change our perspective. Instead of trying to change the situation, we change the way we think about it.

Take failure, for example. Failure—or, more accurately, the fear of it—is one of the biggest reasons why a lot of people don't try something new and potentially risky like asking for a promotion, changing career paths, moving to a new town, starting their own venture, starting a family, or any number of things. It's natural to have anxiety when you think about failing, and when something makes you feel uncomfortable, it's natural to want to avoid it. But what about the notion you have surely heard before that failure is our greatest teacher? If failure causes us to learn our greatest lessons in life, then is it really something we need to avoid at all costs, to the point where the thought of it keeps us from taking risks, putting ourselves out there, or trying something new?

That's reframing, adopting a different and more empowering way of thinking about the same subject. Kendra Scott, founder and CEO of the Kendra Scott jewelry and home goods brand, did this for herself when she set out to create her current business after a difficult failure. When she was just nineteen years old, she decided to forgo college to open a hat store. She was inspired by her stepfather, who was battling brain cancer at the time. Through him she had met a number of people who had lost their hair because of chemotherapy, and she realized there weren't a lot of great headwear options for them. She wanted to remedy that, and she wanted to do so much more. She didn't want to just make hats for people undergoing chemotherapy. She wanted to make hats for everyone.

"I had this big vision," she explained to David when he interviewed her for his podcast. "I was going to open hat stores across the country. Everyone was going to wear hats again, like it was the 1940s." Sadly that didn't happen. She opened one store and tried for five years to make it successful, working seven days a week from morning until night. But in the end, the numbers just didn't add up.

When she had to close her store, it felt like the biggest failure. Her stepfather had just died, and she felt like she had let him and her entire family down. But a few years later, when she started Kendra Scott, she realized that little hat store wasn't so much a failure as it was a great education in how to run a retail business. She was starting her new venture with a solid understanding of margins, overhead, payroll, and so much more. Now she's glad to tell people that story. "I think it's an important thing for entrepreneurs to share their failure stories because they are the bridge to their success. I don't know any entrepreneur that hasn't failed miserably ... [and] hasn't said they're so thankful. It felt horrible in the moment, but now it's like one of the greatest gifts that was ever given."

Failure can cause someone to give up. It can cause someone to doubt themselves or be too embarrassed to admit what happened, but these aren't particularly useful reactions. Coaching yourself through failure means accepting the reality of what happened and finding a way to direct your energy to a positive place so you can move forward. Scott didn't erase her failure; she just adopted a new mind-set about it—a shift in perspective that allowed her to view the same situation in a different light. Later in this book, we will talk more about mistakes and failures, how to plan for (and hopefully avoid) them, and how to recover from them when they happen, but for now we simply want to focus on not allowing the fear of them, or anything else, to get in the way of your belief in yourself. Failures happen—there's no changing that fact—but you can choose to view them as monstrous things you must avoid at all costs, or as moments that are painful but also opportunities. They are opportunities to grow in new and unexpected ways and to learn things you didn't know before, *if* you can coach yourself to stay open to the lessons.

Reframing isn't an exercise in wishful thinking, and it isn't an exercise in denying your feelings. Remember, your feelings are information, clues about what's happening inside your head and what's important to you, so you always want to acknowledge them. Instead, reframing is an exercise in *choosing* a more productive way of thinking about anything you are up against. We don't think it's a stretch to suggest that every experience you have in life is an opportunity to learn and grow if you choose to look for the lesson. David thought about this idea a lot when his wife went through some health challenges. She was diagnosed with juvenile diabetes at the age of seven and has worked to manage the condition her entire life. It was that experience that led the two of them to start The Wendy Novak Diabetes Center at Norton Children's Hospital in Louisville. It was a way of creating something positive out of challenging circumstances.

Then in 2020, in the midst of the COVID-19 crisis, Wendy had a severe diabetic seizure followed by a difficult spinal surgery. It was a really tough time for the whole family, but amid all the stress and worry, David also found a positive side. During a period when it felt like the whole world had been turned upside-down, he and his wife found reason to really focus on each other. He experienced enormous joy in being a partner and helper to her through her recovery process. As a result, their marriage has never been stronger or happier.

Something similar happened with Jason's wife, Elizabeth, when she had to undergo chemotherapy to treat breast cancer. She knew there would be difficult days ahead, but she also knew she didn't want to dread having to go for chemotherapy treatments time after time. So she decided to reframe them as "wellness infusions." She figured it was those treatments that were going to make her well, so why not focus on that outcome above all else? Not only did this help her feel more positive about the experience, but everyone around her picked up on her energy and it changed the whole dynamic of what was happening. Her doctor and nurses began using the same language that she did, and she could feel her positive outlook reflected back at her whenever she went in for treatment.

Reframing is a powerful concept that we will return to time and again throughout this process, and the Take Charge Action that follows will help you practice it in your own life. As you do, the main idea to take away here is that belief is a choice. That's why this section is called "The *Action* of Belief." Belief doesn't just come to you; you have to *actively* choose it.

TAKE CHARGE ACTION:
Change Your *Nots* into *Not Yets*

One of Jason's favorite reframing techniques is to add the word *yet* to the end of a sentence. One of his clients might say to him, "I can't make this shot. It's not possible. I've never made one from this distance before." That might sound reasonable—so reasonable, in fact, that many of us wouldn't think to question whether there's a different way of viewing the situation. But what happens if you add the word *yet* to the end of the last sentence: "I've never made a shot from this distance—*yet.*"

Suddenly it's not so clear that this golfer *can't* make the shot; it's just clear that he or she has never done it before. One small word has changed the equation. "Not done it before" no longer equals "not possible." And that change opens up room for belief to come in. After all, if we think about it, we have all done things in our lives that we have never done before. Lots of things, in fact—we walked for the first time, drove a car for the first time, moved into our own home for the first time, got a job for the first time. Once upon a time we didn't know how to do any of the things we're capable of now. Why can't this become one of those things?

By adding "yet," you turn what could have been the end of a conversation into the beginning of one. If you can't do something, then that's it; there's nothing more to talk about. But if you haven't done something *yet*, then there is a lot more to say and a lot more questions to ask, like "What is it that you need to learn, practice, or do in order to make it happen?"

Try it for yourself:

1) Think of something that is outside your comfort zone. It doesn't have to be about your SBT (remember, we have set that aside for the moment to simply practice getting into a

coaching mindset), unless there's some sabotaging thought about it that is gnawing at you and you can't put it aside. Otherwise, just pick something, anything, that you are unlikely to do. It might be running a marathon. Or, if you're a homebody or hate airplanes, traveling across the world.

2) Frame it in a sentence using *can't* or *not*. For example: "I can't run a marathon" or "It's not possible for me to travel all the way to Australia." Then say the sentence out loud to yourself.

3) Add *yet* to the end of your sentence and then say that out loud: "I can't run a marathon *yet*" or "It is not possible for me to travel all the way to Australia *yet*."

4) Now ask yourself: "What would I need to learn, practice, or do in order to make it happen?" Write down some things that could lead to it becoming a real possibility. Maybe you would get up an hour early each morning and start walking a mile, and then two. Maybe you would research relaxation techniques that are commonly used when someone is afraid to fly. Keep in mind, this doesn't mean you actually have to do the thing you are writing about.

This is just practice. Just see what it's like to view this particular "impossibility" in a different light and imagine what you might do differently if it were possible.

5) Keep this reframing technique handy! As you work through this process, sabotaging thoughts—those *I can'ts* or *it's not possibles*— are likely to come up about the SBT you want to accomplish. When they do, remember reframing, which can help get your mind thinking in a new way. It also can help get your mind thinking in a truer way. After all, none of us are fixed in time. We are all just works in progress, and exactly what we're capable of is an unknown—until we achieve it, that is.

REFRAMING: A DEFINITION

Reframing is a psychological technique that asks us to identify how we view a situation or experience and then change, not the situation or experience, but the way we think about it.

You have to be optimistic. We like to say to "choose optimism and have a plan." It's not just being overly cheery about something. It's about staying positive and thinking about how you can iteratively make progress.

—**TONY XU,** cofounder and CEO, DoorDash

The Practice of Neutrality

When we talk about belief, we're not talking about blind belief or wishful thinking. We aren't suggesting, for example, that a kid who will never grow taller than five feet spend his life trying to get drafted into the NBA. Belief alone is not enough to achieve big things. A *belief in the possible* is what we're aiming for here, but not one that's impervious to reality. It's more like belief paired with an ability to suspend judgment long enough to search for the insights you need to make good decisions. (If you're that five-foot-tall kid, then finding out that the average height for an NBA player during the 2017–2018 season was six-foot-seven[11] is perhaps all the insight you need to make a good decision about whether pursuing the NBA is worth your time.)

Suspending judgment in this way requires a person to stay neutral. Neutrality isn't generally talked about as a state we should aspire to or a skill we should practice. In fact, it isn't talked about much at all in most circles. We tend to value strong opinions and the actions that result from them. Being neutral about something seems like the opposite of those things that we value, but it isn't.

Neutrality is a crucial step on the path to developing *informed* opinions and taking *productive* actions that will lead you where you want to go, rather than just taking action for action's sake. Think back to the definition of the coaching mindset that we just gave you: *Your mind is open to whatever is going to drive your growth or performance, which means avoiding the trap of preconceived notions or prejudging what's going to happen or how.* One of the ways to stay open is to practice approaching situations with a neutral frame of mind, which means with an attitude of "I don't know what's going to happen" or "I don't have all the answers" (which, unless you have some sort of magical, all-knowing, future-seeing powers, is indisputably true).

While David has always believed in keeping an open mind about his career and the challenges he has faced as he rose to leadership positions, he was introduced to the idea of practicing neutrality in an intentional way when he first met Jason. At the time, David was frustrated with his golf game. He felt like he had some talent. He could hit farther than most guys his age, and he could make shots in practice. But when it came to crunch time in tournaments, he would often miss the big shots.

David's friend, Jimmy Dunne, knew he was frustrated, so he suggested he meet with a performance coach he knew who had recently helped take pro golfer Jason Day to number one in the world. That was, of course, Jason. The two met for the first time at a golf club in Florida, and Jason started off their session the same way he does with the professional athletes he coaches—by showing David how to get into a neutral frame of mind before he hit a shot.

He did this by introducing David to a technology he uses called FocusBand, which is essentially a headband that measures your brain frequency while you perform any kind of task. It shows you in real time the state of your brain activity while you do something. Whether stepping up to hit a golf shot or stepping on stage to give a speech—or even when making a big decision about which car to buy or whether to quit your job—human beings perform best when they are in a calm state characterized by lower brain frequencies, rather than the over-stimulated, high-beta frequencies that most of us experience far too often in our busy, stress-filled lives.

Through the FocusBand, David could see right away that he was often in an agitated state when he stepped up to hit the ball. He could also see what worked to slow things down and move him to a lower brain frequency. Some calming breaths, a shift in focus, and he found he was able to change his mental state.

A neutral state means *not* feeling anxious or fearful, *not* feeling overly excited or overthinking what you're about to do, *not* feeling uncomfortable or self-conscious. When you think about it this way, you can imagine how useful it could be well beyond the golf course. Getting into a neutral state is about emptying your mind of all the distracting or sabotaging thoughts that can get in the way so that you can proceed from that neutral place.

Once you have emptied your mind of those kinds of thoughts, you can simply focus on being present, on noticing what's happening in the moment and letting it unfold. You can then accept what's happening and respond to it with a clear head. Imagine how useful that could be when your anxiety rises before a job interview, when you're pitching investors or a new client, when you're receiving feedback about your performance or proposal, when you're having a difficult conversation with someone you care about, before giving a speech or presentation, or really anytime that you put yourself out there to be judged or rejected or to try something you might not succeed at.

You don't need Jason's FocusBand technology to get the hang of it either. The following are some actions you can take to practice getting into a neutral frame of mind.

TAKE CHARGE ACTION:
Practice Detachment Breathing

1) Call to mind an experience that caused you to have a negative reaction. It could be an insulting or hurtful thing someone said to you, a public failure at work, or something similar.

2) Sit with the thought long enough that you can really feel the emotions you experienced when the event happened.

3) Now, close your eyes and shift your attention to your breath. Focus on the rhythm of your breathing as the air flows in and out, in and out, in and out. Do this for five to ten breaths.

4) Open your eyes and notice what happened to the negative thoughts and feelings. While you were focused on your breathing, did they disappear from your mind?

The purpose of this exercise is to remind us that we have more control over our state of mind than we give ourselves credit for. The negative feelings attached to an experience can recede, often rather quickly, when we shift our focus away from them to something neutral like our breath. It's like starving the negative thought of energy by choosing to focus our mind elsewhere.

We suggest you practice this now so you can get the hang of how it feels. Once you are familiar with it, you can use it anytime, anywhere, when you notice yourself getting anxious, upset, or having thoughts that depreciate your confidence or self-worth. Then, once you have calmed your energy, you can be more present in the moment, accept what is happening, and respond with a clearer head.

● ● ● ● ● ● ● ●

TAKE CHARGE ACTION:
Put Yourself in a Neutral State

Neutrality is something we recommend people practice on a regular basis, and not just before they are ready to step into a high-pressure situation. The idea is to master the ability before you need it. Being able to put yourself in a neutral state allows you to perform better. It allows you to quiet all the chatter in your head and focus on the task at hand.

People use different methods to achieve this. Here are some options that have worked for us and for others. It doesn't matter so much which method you choose, but that it works for you and that you do it regularly!

1) Meditation: Jason practices meditation regularly, as do lots of highly successful people like Arianna Huffington, the late Kobe Bryant, and Starbucks CEO Kevin Johnson, who learned the practice from Ringo Starr!

2) Journaling: David writes in a gratitude journal every morning about what he's thankful for. You can try this or a more traditional form of journaling where you simply record what's on your mind. Julia Cameron, author of the book *The Artist's Way*, started a popular practice of writing what she called "morning pages"— three pages of spontaneous writing first thing each morning on whatever comes to mind.[12]

3) Prayer or regular periods of quiet contemplation.

4) Conscious breathing: Jason uses another breathing practice, which is similar to the one above, several times a day, every day. At random times when the thought occurs to him, he pauses and takes conscious breaths. He focuses only on counting his breaths, up to 10 at a time. It takes less than a minute and it helps him recognize the state he's currently in and then move to a calmer, more present, more neutral one. He often wears a rubber band on his wrist to remind himself to do this. Every time he notices the rubber band, it serves as a reminder to breathe consciously.

SELF-COACHING TIP: If you had difficulty answering any of the questions from the first chapter, try using the detachment breathing or conscious breathing exercise to get yourself into a neutral state. Then go back to the questions and see if it's easier to answer them when you are in a calmer, more present frame of mind.

Harnessing Your Awareness

Once you have quieted your mind and gotten into a neutral state, that's when you can really listen to yourself and make good decisions. You can start to harness your awareness, which for our purposes here, we define as an ability to do two things: 1) to become conscious of what your mind is focused on at any given moment, and 2) to shift that focus where you want it to go.

What can make this so difficult is that we all have default ways of thinking and those defaults drive our actions most of the time. What's more, most of us tend to hold on to those defaults, following their lead even when it's clear that they're not leading us where we want to go.

David once interviewed hockey legend and six-time Stanley Cup champion Mark Messier, who told him a story about when he first came to play with the New York Rangers. Messier had already achieved plenty of success playing with the Edmonton Oilers, which was why he was so surprised to discover how different things were at his new club. The Oilers had always played to win, but there was a different culture at the Rangers. This was 1991, and the team hadn't won the Stanley Cup since 1940. Among New Yorkers, this long losing streak was known as *the curse*.

Of course the curse wasn't real, but Messier found that many in the organization acted as if it was—it was their default way of thinking. "There was a sense of not wanting to talk about winning the Stanley Cup for the fact that we were going to put too much pressure on everybody," Messier explained. "That was the craziest thing I ever heard ... I don't think you can be successful if you don't want to talk about it, and if you don't create the vision and roadmap for how you're going to get there."

In Messier's third year with the Rangers, a new head coach, Mike Keenan, was brought in and he and Messier held similar views on the subject. Keenan made the team watch tapes of ticker-tape parades thrown for past winners so the team could start to imagine themselves as winners too, instead of feeling cursed to be inevitable losers. Messier described it as the start of a process of changing "that internal dialog that is so critical to the way you think of yourself as a person."

Once you have quieted your mind and gotten into a neutral state, then you have a much better chance of becoming aware of ways of thinking that may not be working for you. Once you gain that awareness, then you can choose to direct your focus elsewhere.

This is a skill that's useful in many contexts. David once interviewed Ryan Serhant, New York real estate broker and star of the television series *Million Dollar Listing*. Serhant described a list-making exercise he uses when he gets anxious or overly focused on the negative. He writes a list of everything he's imagining about a challenging situation. This allows him to become more aware of where his mind is currently focused. Then, to shift his focus to a more positive place, he makes a second list of all the good things he can imagine that could result from the same situation. He used the example of talking to strangers at a party. He considers himself pretty introverted by nature, so that kind of situation can make him feel quite nervous.

"It's amazing what happens when you just sit down with a pen and paper," Serhant explained. "[It can] plant the seeds in people's brains about what they can do." (The next Take Charge Action follows Serhant's approach.)

Serhant came up with this tactic because, as he explained, "It's easy to focus on negative thoughts." What he describes is a good example of something that researchers call negativity bias. S. Shyam Sundar, distinguished professor of communication and co-director of the Media Effects Research Lab at Penn State, described it this way: "The negativity bias suggests that individuals may be more likely to recall and be persuaded by negative information, rather than positive information. Positive news—when good things happen—doesn't seem to be as memorable for us compared to when something negative happens."[13]

Negativity bias may be something that we are hardwired for as human beings, but that doesn't mean we are at its mercy. When we are aware of it, we can do something about it. The main thing to take away here is that we often have more power than we give ourselves credit for, not to control exactly, but to shift or guide our thinking where we want it to go, to choose a more positive outlook or a more productive frame of mind. But it all starts with becoming aware of how you are thinking, rather than acting on autopilot. Once again, this is something we can practice and the following Take Charge Actions will help.

TAKE CHARGE ACTION:
Shift Your Focus

1) Spend a few moments thinking about a situation that makes you feel anxious, frustrated, or fearful.

2) Make a list of every negative thing you can imagine happening as a result of the situation. For example, in Ryan Serhant's scenario of being too nervous to talk to strangers at a party, he might have written something like: *If I try to talk to them, they will ignore me. Or laugh at me. Or think I'm stupid or boring. Or get annoyed at me because I'm interrupting their conversation.*

3) Turn the page and make a new list, this time of every positive thing you can imagine

happening as a result of the same situation. To use the same example, Serhant could have written: *If I try to talk to them, I might make some new business contacts. I might learn something new. I might hear something interesting. I might make a new friend. I might enjoy this party more.*

4) Sit back and notice how it's possible to shift your feelings about something by changing your focus, even though the facts of the situation haven't changed. We all have it within our power to do this for ourselves.

• • • • • • • •

TAKE CHARGE ACTION:
Balance Your Negatives with Positives

It's possible to do more than just shift our feelings about a difficult situation we find ourselves in. When we are aware and intentional about it, we can also shift our feelings about ourselves. When anxious or negative thoughts threaten to derail your belief in yourself or what you want to accomplish, try making "bad" lists and "good" lists, as follows:

1) Don't just let negative thoughts about yourself swirl around in your head. Bring your awareness to them and capture them on the page by making a "bad" list of all the things you consider to be potential drawbacks or weaknesses that might keep you from succeeding.

2) But don't stop there. To help shift your focus, make a "good" list right next to the bad one of all your assets and positive qualities that can, or already have, helped you succeed in different areas of your life. Think broadly about your skills, personality traits (your sense of humor? your resilience?), experiences, relationships, and anything else you have on your side.

3) Once you have finished your lists, try taking this exercise to the next level by revisiting your "bad" list and *reframing* each of the items on it by choosing a more productive interpretation. "I don't have enough financial knowledge to open my own business" could

become "I don't have enough financial knowledge *yet.*" Or, reframe this same negative as
a source of potential opportunities: "I don't
have enough financial ability, so I could find
the right person to partner with, hire someone
who will complement my skills, or gain more
experience to broaden my financial abilities."

Like reframing, this list-making technique is one that
you will want to keep at the ready throughout this process for whenever sabotaging thoughts arise. It will
help you balance any negative thoughts with a positive counterweight.

Build Your Self-Knowledge

In the last chapter, we talked about the fact that it's hard to
coach someone you don't know, which is one of the reasons
why we began by asking you questions about yourself to
deepen your self-knowledge. This is an ongoing process—one,
in fact, that never ends—which is crucial to success. David
once summarized his path to achievement this way: self-
assessment, self-improvement, success, self-assessment,
self-improvement, success. And on and on, continuing to this
day.

THE SELF-COACHING MINDSET

Knowing yourself is crucial to your growth and development, but it can be challenging. Benjamin Franklin once wrote in his *Poor Richard's Almanack*, "There are three things extremely hard: steel, a diamond, and to know one's self."[14] Challenging though it may be, research backs up the importance of making the effort. A solid foundation of self-awareness turns out to be a pretty good indicator of personal success. Summarizing a mountain of research on the subject, organizational psychologist Tasha Eurich wrote in her book *Insight* that self-awareness is "necessary to our survival and success—at work, in our relationships, and in life. There is strong scientific evidence that people who know themselves and how others see them are happier. They make smarter decisions. They have better personal and professional relationships. They raise more mature children. They're smarter, superior students who choose better careers. They're more creative, more confident, and better communicators. They're less aggressive and less likely to lie, cheat, and steal. They're better performers at work who get more promotions. They're more effective leaders with more enthusiastic employees. They even lead more profitable companies."[15]

Surely there is reason enough in that one statement to motivate practically everyone, so we continue here with more ways to help you build your self-knowledge. Remembering to set aside your SBT until the next chapter, let's spend some time thinking about what is most important to you and what drives you. These can be big questions for some of us. We suggested earlier that if you had trouble answering the questions in the last chapter, you could try calming your mind and getting into a neutral state before trying again. The same advice applies here. Try one of the breathing techniques—or meditate, journal, or pray if you have already developed one of those as a regular practice—and then approach these big questions about yourself from a neutral and present frame of mind. And remember: You don't have to have crystal-clear answers to get something out of the exercise. You can always come back and refine your answers as your self-knowledge deepens through this process. You only need to do the best you can with the knowledge you have now and go from there.

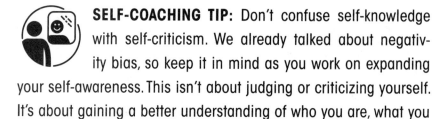

SELF-COACHING TIP: Don't confuse self-knowledge with self-criticism. We already talked about negativity bias, so keep it in mind as you work on expanding your self-awareness. This isn't about judging or criticizing yourself. It's about gaining a better understanding of who you are, what you want, and what motivates you as a unique individual.

TAKE CHARGE ACTION:
Prioritize What You Value Most

Have you ever considered what values drive your decisions and behavior? You are guided by these principles and convictions whether you know it or not. Identifying what they are will give you a better understanding of how to make choices and whether you are making the right choices *for you*.

1) To identify the values that are most important to you, read through the list below. Put a check mark next to the ones that feel *important*. Put two check marks next to ones that feel *very important*. Feel free to add to the list if important values come to mind that aren't listed here.

ACCOUNTABILITY	LEARNING
ADVANCEMENT	LOVE
AUTHENTICITY	LOYALTY
COMPASSION	PATIENCE
COOPERATION	PEACE
CREATIVITY	POWER
EMPATHY	PROFESSIONALISM
FAITH	RECOGNITION
FAMILY	RESPECT
FORGIVENESS	RESPONSIBILITY
FREEDOM	SECURITY
FUN	SERVICE
GROWTH	SUCCESS
HELPFULNESS	TRUSTWORTHINESS
HONESTY	TRUTH
INDEPENDENCE	WEALTH
INTEGRITY	WISDOM
KINDNESS	

2) Focus on the values you checked off twice, the ones that are *very important* to you. Pick your top five or six and write them down. These are the values you can't live without.

One of the things that I've seen in our students, and I think in all human beings, is a need to find real purpose in their lives, and a need to find a way to put that into practice.

—**MARGARET DUFFY,** professor of strategic communication, Missouri School of Journalism

TAKE CHARGE ACTION:
Define Your Purpose

Your Single Biggest Thing is what you want to accomplish in your life right now. Your purpose is different; it is what you contribute to the world. It's likely to last long after you've accomplished your current SBT and your future SBTs. Simon Sinek, bestselling author of *Start with Why*, believes every person and every company needs to have a purpose behind what they do. He writes, "Very few people or companies can clearly articulate WHY they do WHAT they do. By WHY I mean your purpose, cause or belief—WHY does your company exist? WHY do you get out of bed every morning? And WHY should anyone care?"[16]

Your SBT and your purpose may sound similar or they may not. (In the next chapter, we will ask you to compare the two to make sure they aren't in conflict.) Use the following steps to help you create a purpose statement. Or, if you already have one, use these steps to make sure it still resonates for you.

1) Your purpose should be something you feel positive about, so look back at your Joy Builder list for clues. What brings you joy and energizes you?

2) Your purpose should be something that compels you to act. Is there something that you need or feel called to do?

3) Your purpose should be something you're good at. Ask yourself what you excel at. What comes naturally to you?

4) Your purpose should be other-directed. Ask yourself what other people appreciate most about you. How do you help them? How do you contribute to their lives?

5) Your purpose statement may or may not reflect what you do for a living, so think broadly about the answers to these questions and let those answers reflect what's most meaningful to you. When Oprah Winfrey was young, her purpose was "to be a teacher. And to be known for inspiring my students to be more than they thought they could be."[17] Her aspiration then was to become a school teacher. She didn't yet know that the television airwaves would become her "classroom," but when she eventually started her famous talk show, her purpose statement still fit.

6) Consider what you have come up with so far, and then take a stab at writing a short but meaningful purpose statement that reflects these things.

7) Read it back and make revisions as it feels right to you. Let it sit for a while, reread it, and revise it again as necessary.

8) Write your purpose statement on a sticky note in pencil. We may evolve our purpose as we grow and learn. We may want to refine how it's phrased. That's fine. Just like us, it's a work in progress. Let it be just that, but don't underestimate its value just because it isn't written in stone.

The values and purpose you defined here will be important moving forward because they will serve as guardrails as you continue your journey, helping to guide your decisions as you actively coach yourself toward your SBT. Consider posting them in a prominent place alongside your SBT so you can't help but look at them often.

Jason's Values

Forgiveness, kindness, truth, peace, courage, freedom, and love

Jason's Purpose

To help others become the best version of themselves because in serving others, I serve myself.

David's Values

Faith in God, family, belief in all people, recognition, learning, and giving back

David's Purpose

To make the world a better place by developing better leaders.

EXAMPLES OF PURPOSE STATEMENTS

- To become a respected thought leader who makes unique contributions to my field.
- To create work that inspires people to think differently.
- To build a stable and loving home environment where my children will thrive and reach their full potential.
- To lead a company where people love to come to work every day and feel recognized for their contributions.
- To work each day toward making my community a better place to live—for my family, myself, and all my neighbors.
- To become the kind of person who others seek out for coaching and advice.

3

The Self-Coaching Plan

Uncover Transformational Insights

• • • • • • • •

Your Self-Coaching Plan Toolkit

 Make Your Journey a Purposeful One

 Practice Your Humility

 Consult Your Assistant Coaches

 Kickstart Your Learning Curve

 Identify How You Handle Roadblocks

 Listen to What Your Single Biggest Thing Is Telling You

A moment's insight is sometimes worth a lifetime's experience.

—OLIVER WENDELL HOLMES, SR., American physician and poet[18]

It's time to return to that destination you set for yourself in the first chapter of this book—your Single Biggest Thing. You have defined where you want to go, but having a destination is not the same as knowing how to get there. What do you do first? What do you do next? What could stand in your way? These are the kinds of insights you need in order to figure out how to get from where you are now to where you want to go.

Take Jason's journey, for example. He thought he was on the right path when he left his position at the boat charter company and got into real estate, but then he found himself miserable in his new career. He had to figure out: What was making him miserable? What had gone wrong with the new career he had chosen? What should he be doing instead? He needed some insight into himself and what he really wanted.

David knew he felt more joy in his work when he was able to pursue his own vision and see where it took him and the company he worked for. For that to happen on a larger scale, he knew he had to be the one in charge. That translated into a desire to run something someday, but there was a recurring problem that could have kept him from rising to that level: his fear of public speaking. For years he would speak in front of audiences at meetings and conferences because he knew he had to, but he never felt like he was doing it all that well. How was he going to lead an organization if he couldn't get up in front of people and educate or inspire them? He had to figure out: How could he get past his discomfort on stage? What did he need to do to improve his abilities? He needed some insight into how to gain the skills and perspective he was lacking.

So how do you do something like that? How do you gain the insights you need to figure out what to do to reach your destination and how to handle the roadblocks that get in your way? That's what we're going to start figuring out right now.

Make Sure Your Destination Is Purposeful

First things first: We are going to ask you to take another look at your SBT with that open coaching mindset we introduced in Chapter 2 and see how it holds up against the values and purpose you defined for yourself. If it doesn't hold up, that should provide some insight into where you have work to do.

When Jason found himself miserable after changing careers and moving to a new town, he had to figure out what had gone wrong. One of the things he discovered was that he had never taken the time to think about what his real true values and purpose were. He had mostly focused on the narrow goal of making ends meet. That's important, surely, but there are all sorts of ways to make a living, and the ways Jason had chosen weren't bringing him joy.

When Jason finally sat down and defined his values and purpose, it became clear that they revolved around the idea of serving other people. That was what made him feel alive and truly useful. That clarity made him realize that his real estate career didn't match his values and purpose. What he needed was a new destination that felt more purposeful and aligned with his values. That discovery led him to his next career, and if he hadn't had the insight, he might never have become the performance coach he is today.

The key thing here is to make sure—to the best of your abilities with what you know right now—that the destination you will be working toward is worth your time and effort. Sometimes we set our sights on something because it's what we think we should be doing or because someone else thinks it's what we should accomplish. That kind of destination is going to be a lot harder to reach than one that feels purposeful and brings you joy along the way. So let's take a moment to check in and try to find alignment between who we are and what we plan to do. The following exercise will help.

TAKE CHARGE ACTION:
Make Your Journey a Purposeful One

1) Divide a page into two columns. On the left side of the page, write down your SBT at the top.

2) On the right side, write down your purpose. List your values underneath.

3) Read your SBT aloud to yourself and compare it to your purpose and values. Ask yourself: Do they support one another? Are they compatible? Do they feel at odds? For example, you might have written "Become regional manager" as your SBT, a position that requires long hours at the office and lots of travel. But if you also chose freedom and family as top values, then you have to ask yourself if those conflict with your destination. How will long working hours offer you freedom? How will travel away from home impact your family? (There may be good answers to these questions, but make sure you know what they are.)

4) If your SBT feels aligned with your purpose and values, then great! Keep reading.

5) If not, then ask yourself why not. And make adjustments as needed.

ADDITIONAL TACTIC TO TRY:

- To figure out what adjustments to make, you can try revisiting your Joy Builder and Joy Blocker lists. You might find clues there about why your destination doesn't feel like it matches your purpose and values. You might also ask yourself which feels more joyful? Does the idea of achieving your SBT feel joyful? Does the idea of living up to your values and purpose feel joyful? If the answer to either question is no, then that could be a clue about which answers you need to revisit.

Stay Open to Insights

In this chapter, we're going to take you through some tactics for discovering the insights you need to move closer to your destination, but first it's important to make sure you're open to receiving them. We shut ourselves off to the insights that could help us grow and achieve more all the time. We don't do it consciously, not usually. We do it because we're busy or overwhelmed and just not paying attention. Or because we're afraid of change or failure. Or because the insight makes us feel uncomfortable and we don't know what to do with it. It takes effort and intention to stay open to new insights about ourselves and what we want for our lives and careers.

David has interviewed dozens of people who have been highly successful in a wide variety of fields for his podcast, "How Leaders Lead," and he has found there's a consistent set of traits that have helped just about every one of them achieve big things—with two main ones that stand out: 1) they display a healthy dose of humility, and 2) they are all avid learners.

We will come back to that second trait later in this chapter, but first let's focus on humility, by which we mean an ability to keep your ego in check and accept that you (along with every other person on this planet) are less than perfect and capable of making mistakes—and that's okay. In the age of social media, where people like to tweet their every thought and Instagram what they had for breakfast, humility isn't the most talked-about subject these days. But maybe it should be. Research shows that people who are humble report higher levels of well-being, both physical and mental, and are better able to manage stress.[19] For our purposes here, humility is especially useful in helping people stay open to the kind of insights they need to grow, learn, and get better at what they do.

That's because humility means being able to admit that you don't know all the answers, which is the first step in finding them. It means being able to admit that you make mistakes, which is the first step in correcting them and avoiding them the next time. It means being able to admit, without crippling judgment, that there is always room to grow, learn, and do better. It means being honest with yourself first, and then with others you trust, about the things that could be holding you back. It means saying to yourself that you can't do it alone, that you need other people. You can begin to see how humility is essential to a coaching mindset. And when you lead with your humility, profound insights can come your way even when you're not looking for them.

Jason discovered that one day on the golf course when he was playing a round with someone he had never met before. When Jason learned as a child that he had dyslexia, it was something he often felt like he needed to hide. He'd been working for a long time to get more comfortable with this fact about himself, which was how he ended up talking about it that day with a virtual stranger. And it was a good thing that he did. When his playing partner found out about Jason's dyslexia, he said something that has stuck with Jason ever since: "My daughter is dyslexic too, and you know what? It really helped her to figure out that it just means that her brain works differently. It's not wrong. It just works in a different way. There are so many successful people in the world who are wired differently. It allows them to see things or do things that other people aren't able to see or do because their brains are unique in that way."

Jason had never thought about his dyslexia that way before, so it was a light-bulb moment for him. His whole life he had considered it to be a curse, something he had to hide or at least compensate for. Suddenly he started thinking it could be his superpower—one of the things that made him unique and able to process the world in a different and advantageous way.

By choosing to be open about his dyslexia, and with a stranger no less, Jason was able to receive a profound insight, a way to *reframe* his dyslexia, which would change the way he thought of himself from then on. And that moment might never have happened if he hadn't had the humility, and the courage, to be open and honest about it.

As you strive to reach your destination in the coming pages and as you confront the challenges that will come up along the way, humility can be your friend and guide. Humility, incidentally, like so many other things we have talked about (belief, neutrality, and so on), is something you can cultivate and practice. You don't need to leave these things up to chance!

One way to cultivate humility is to realize that whatever successes you have had in life (and we are sure there have been many), there isn't a single one that you can take full and complete credit for. Surely there has been someone, and probably many someones, who have provided you help, resources, knowledge, advice, time, energy, goodwill, inspiration, support, and so much more. The same is going to be true as you strive to reach your new destination.

When David was CEO of Yum! Brands, he learned a lot about this subject from John Wooden, whose coaching mindset we highlighted in Chapter 2. This was a man who knew how to bring out top-notch performances, and humility was a big part of his core teachings to the young athletes who came through his program.

Coach Wooden set an expectation for every one of his players that whenever someone scored, he had to acknowledge whoever gave him the assist. The scorer could choose how he wanted to recognize the person—by pointing to him, giving him a high-five, and so on—but the important thing was to focus on who had helped him succeed, not on his own success.

When you do something like this, it's as much for you as it is for the other person. It creates a shift in perspective—in this case, the scoring player shifts from focusing on himself to focusing outwardly on his teammates and what's happening around him. That perspective shift can be useful when you're searching for the insights you need to achieve new things.

Of course practicing humility in this way has a positive effect on the people around you too—the same people who can help you succeed. Once a player asked Wooden,

"Coach, what if the guy isn't looking when I call him out?"

"Oh, he'll be looking," Wooden assured him. After all, who among us doesn't like to be acknowledged for what we do?

TAKE CHARGE ACTION:
Practice Your Humility

Let's take a page from Coach Wooden's playbook and set an expectation for ourselves to humbly acknowledge the fact that we would not be able to accomplish what we accomplish in life without the contributions of others. Use the following steps to start practicing humility now so you can benefit from it and the perspective it affords you throughout this process.

1) Think about a recent win you experienced in your career or in any aspect of your life. Take a moment to acknowledge the fact that that win was not yours alone by listing all the people who helped you achieve it.

2) Include a brief description of how each person on your list contributed to your success, either directly or indirectly.

3) Next, take your humility practice a step further by grounding it in gratitude. Do something tangible to acknowledge the assist. Write thank you notes to the people you listed or call out their contributions in your next meeting. Not only will this help you cultivate humility by acknowledging publicly how others have helped you, but it will also inspire the people around you to provide you with even more assists in the future.

4) Now, think of a setback or challenge you have experienced and repeat the process. Who had your back? Who supported you through it? Who listened to you vent? Who picked you back up and inspired you to keep going? Make a separate list of their names and ask yourself if you ever said *thank you*. If not, maybe now is the time. If so, maybe it's time to say it again!

5) Finally, make an effort to do this more often in your life in real time.

I mean, just be humble ... We're all a mix of confidence and inse-curity, and, you know, it's okay to be insecure about things and to try to address them. So much of the work of being a better leader at this point is now internal work: How do I work through issues within myself that I want to address? The better I can do that, the more effective I'll be.

—**ETHAN BROWN,** founder and CEO, Beyond Meat

Learn to Ask for Insights

As we pointed out in the introduction to this book, coach-ing yourself doesn't mean you have to go it alone or come up with all the answers yourself. It just means that *you* take responsibility for seeking the insights you need and using them to move yourself forward.

One of the best tactics you can use to start gaining insights into how to reach your destination is to ask for them from people who have done something similar or simply from people you admire and respect. For example, if you're look-ing to start a new business, you can seek out entrepreneurs you admire. If you have a health challenge, you can talk to someone who has been through something similar. You can also ask for insights when you're dealing with less spe-cific challenges that might be getting in your way, like when you're feeling stuck or uncertain. Collecting outside opinions is a great place to start when you're not sure what to do next.

A friend recently asked David if he would give some advice to his son who had just started his career at an investment bank and was struggling. David agreed and talked on the phone with the son, asking him questions about what his job was like and how he felt about the people he worked with. As David listened to the answers, another important question came to mind. Finally he asked the young man, "Do you really love working in finance?"

The young man thought for a moment. "Well, everyone in my family is either a doctor or they're in finance," he slowly answered. "I didn't want to become a doctor, and I'm good at finance."

Of course that's not the same as *loving* what he did. There was no joy in his answer. As they talked more, it turned out that it had never occurred to him to ask himself these kinds of questions when it came to his career: What do you love? What brings you joy? What energizes you? What makes you feel purposeful?

Through further conversation, David helped him figure out that he might prefer to be in management instead of finance. That was something David was able to help him diagnose because he has a broad depth of experience running companies and overseeing a wide range of disciplines that contribute to those companies. At that early stage in his life, this young man had only been exposed to two options: finance and medicine. So when David starting talking to him about other things he might want to do, the information really resonated with him.

David had a similar conversation with a woman who was feeling stuck in her career. She was working in the finance department at her company under a boss who was head of investor relations. When David asked her what she wanted to do, she had a clear vision of her SBT: "I want my boss's job. I want to be head of investor relations."

"Well, is your boss looking to leave or retire?"

"Not anytime soon," she answered.

"Well, if there isn't an opportunity there, are they offering you anything else? Are they doing anything to make sure you stick around?"

"There aren't a lot of women in the company, so they want me to stay. The president suggested I could become his chief of staff since I can't be head of investor relations."

"What would it mean to become his chief of staff?"

"I really don't know."

It was starting to sound to David like the options weren't so great at her current company, like they were offering her a new title just to please her but without putting much behind it. So he decided to take a different tack.

"Have you gotten any calls from other firms or from headhunters?"

"I have actually."

"What sort of positions have they been calling about?"

"Head of investor relations."

If she was getting calls like that, it was clear to David that people already saw her as capable of handling the position she wanted. So, instead of asking herself whether she should leave her current company, David suggested she frame the question a bit differently.

"Go back to the president of your company and get him to define exactly what is meant by this chief of staff position they're offering you. And then call back those places that have contacted you about jobs and find out more. That way you can really compare what your options are and choose the best one."

That's what the woman did. She decided her company wasn't doing enough to keep her, so she moved on to the position she wanted. She took a job running investor relations at another firm because, as scary as it was to leave the place where she'd worked for so long, the challenge of that new position was what she wanted most.

Of course that was an insight she figured out for herself. David just asked her some questions and gave her some perspective that helped clarify things for her. It's important to remember, however, that not all insights are created equal. When you ask for help or advice, you may get answers that range in terms of their usefulness to you. That's okay. Think of the people you ask as your assistant coaches. You will consult them, you will listen to them with humility and an open coaching mindset, but when it comes time to make a decision about what to do, you're the head coach. Only you get to make the call.

SELF-COACHING TIP: If you're someone who's uncomfortable asking for help, try returning to the *reframing* technique, which asks us to change, not the situation, but the way we think about it. So, rather than focusing on your discomfort, ask yourself this question: *Do I enjoy helping people?* Most of us will readily say yes. Being helpful generally makes us feel valued and useful. If that's true, then ask yourself a second question: *If I enjoy helping others, then why wouldn't someone enjoy helping me?* If you're respectful and appreciative, most people will gladly help if they can. And if someone turns you down, just remember that there are still lots of people out there who would be happy to help, just as you would be happy to help them.

TAKE CHARGE ACTION:
Consult Your Assistant Coaches

Take a look at your SBT. What is the first thing that comes to mind that you *don't know* about it? The answer may be something as broad as "how to get started." It may be something about the destination itself and what it might take to get there. Or it may be about you—your strengths and weaknesses and how they will help or inhibit your progress.

You are now going to start collecting opinions about what you can do to turn your "don't knows" into insights to move you forward:

1) **Who to ask:** Start by making a list of three to five people you can talk to about what you want to achieve. You might start with a friend or family member, a boss or coworker, or someone who has achieved something similar. Choose people you believe will be encouraging, honest, or both. You might want to choose a backup option or two as well. Most people will be glad to offer their advice and perspective, but sometimes people will say no. Don't take it personally if this happens. There will always be someone else you can ask!

2) **How to ask:** Remember to be mindful of the person's time. Start by asking if he or she is willing to give you some advice, and if the answer is yes, come prepared with a short description of what you're looking to accomplish. Also prepare a short description of why you are asking this particular person, for example, "I know you went through something

similar" or "I've noticed you always have such good advice for people in this area."

3) **What to ask**: David's favorite question for people is always "What would you do if you were me?" If you're looking for insight into a specific aspect of your SBT, say so: "I'm struggling to get started and I wondered if you had any suggestions?"

4) **Keep a record**: Don't forget to make notes about people's comments so you can continue to reflect on them. And don't forget to compare any insights you get to your purpose and values. Remember that these things are meant to act as guardrails to keep you on track so consult them often.

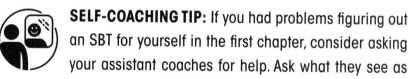

SELF-COACHING TIP: If you had problems figuring out an SBT for yourself in the first chapter, consider asking your assistant coaches for help. Ask what they see as your strengths and what long- or short-term goals they think could help you grow yourself or your career. Compare the answers you get and see what resonates for you personally. And don't forget, the thought of achieving your SBT should bring you joy!

What to Do with Unwanted Insights

Just because you ask someone for their insights doesn't mean you have to take their advice or adopt their opinions. No one except you can decide whether the advice is good and worth following.

If you find yourself having doubts or even getting upset about an insight someone has shared, remember your coaching mindset and take some time to become more aware. Be curious about your reaction rather than just rejecting the insight outright. Are you feeling that way because it wasn't the right advice for you? Or is there something else getting in the way of your accepting sound advice?

When David was the head of marketing at the Pepsi-Cola Company, his SBT was to one day become president of one of PepsiCo's divisions. It didn't matter to him which one; he just knew he wanted the experience of running something someday. When he told that to Wayne Callaway, then Chairman of PepsiCo, Callaway's response wasn't exactly what David was hoping for.

"David," Callaway said to him, "you're a really good marketing guy."

"But Wayne, I really want to be president of a division."

"David," Callaway said again, "you're a really, *really* good marketing guy."

It was a frustrating response. David would have liked for Callaway to support his vision for his future wholeheartedly. But once David accepted his frustration and started to question where it was coming from, it got him thinking differently. Clearly people like Callaway weren't seeing David the way he wanted to be seen, which was as someone with a broad range of skills that went far beyond marketing. Instead of blaming Callaway for that, he began to think about how he could get the people whose support he would need to see his potential as a future division president.

If David had used one of our reframing exercises at that moment, he might have done something like this: "Wayne thinks I'm a talented marketer, but he doesn't see me as president material" could be reframed as "Wayne thinks I'm a talented marketer, but he doesn't see me as president material *yet.*" The question would then become: What did David need to do to be seen the way he wanted?

Not long after that encounter, an opening came up for chief operating officer at Pepsi-Cola Company. David didn't have any operating experience, but he went to his boss, Craig Weatherup, and begged him for the job, making the case that he could step into the new role and get quickly up to speed despite his lack of operational experience. And if he couldn't, he told Weatherup to send him back to marketing—or even fire him, if that's what he thought was best. That's how much he wanted the job.

David got the job and worked his tail off at it. He was able to learn a new aspect of the business and have a positive impact. And the experience put him on track to become a division president and even CEO. He was no longer just a marketing guy. The insight that led him down that path came because he asked for advice from someone he respected, but he didn't just take that advice at face value and he didn't just reject it out of hand when it wasn't what he wanted to hear.

When you come up against insights that are unwanted or cause you to feel resistance, a good tactic is to simply pause and use one of your methods for getting into a neutral state. Any advice, feedback, or insight is best processed when you're in a neutral frame of mind. It will help you to be more open and less reactive, and it will help you to analyze the potential benefits or drawbacks of something without your feelings, fears, or anxieties getting in the way.

What's more, any insights you get that you're unsure about should be measured against your values and purpose. In fact, any insights of any kind should be measured against your values and purpose, even if you feel good about them. There's a difference between good advice and good advice *for you*. The young man David mentored, for example, may have gotten good advice in his life about how to pursue a career in finance from family members who had followed that path before him. However, if finance wasn't where his heart was, then that wasn't good advice *for him*.

Become an Avid Learner

You can still gain insights from others even when you can't ask them directly for advice. This comes back to the second of the two qualities David sees most often in the successful leaders he interviews for his podcast: They are avid learners who are constantly on the lookout for new ideas and insights and consult a wide range of sources to find them. In fact, that's one of the main reasons David started his podcast—so he could learn from the great leaders he gets to talk to and help others learn from them as well.

One such interview came from Frank Blake, former CEO of Home Depot, who describes himself as someone who was a highly unlikely candidate for that position. He had been a lawyer, working in mergers and acquisitions for the company, when Ken Langone, a representative from the board of directors, called him up and offered him the job of CEO. Blake was shocked. It wasn't a position he had been aiming for or even considered. "It never occurred to me that I would be the CEO," Blake admitted.

He was so shocked, in fact, that he didn't say yes right away. He said he needed a day to think about it, and he told the board that they should think about it, too. "You might need someone with deeper retail experience than I have," he said to them.

A day later they still wanted him, and he was intrigued enough by the challenge that he said yes. So there he was, someone with a lawyer's background stepping into a retail business with 350,000 employees looking to him to lead. He describes his first year as the unlikely CEO as a "crash course in leadership."

"I read a lot. I looked at examples of leadership. I became a real student of leadership. It wasn't really anything I'd focused on before in my life…. I think I'm proof that leadership can be learned." He even went to his son for advice. An Iraq War veteran who was working as a store manager at Home Depot at the time, his son had some of the leadership experience Blake was lacking. When it came time for Blake to address all those hundreds of thousands of employees for the first time, he called his son to get some insight about what he should say.

"I can tell you how I start weekly store meetings," Blake's son responded. "I read from Bernie Marcus and Arthur Blank's *Built from Scratch*." The book, written by the founders of Home Depot, is a great entrepreneurial story that talks about many of the values that built and sustained the company. Blake thought it was a great idea, so for his first address to the company as CEO, he read a passage from the book about the concept of the inverted pyramid—an organizational structure where front-line employees, considered the top of the pyramid, are empowered to take more ownership, while leadership remains at the bottom to support and prop them up. It perfectly embodied Blake's vision for how he wanted to lead the company.

When Jason first decided he wanted to become a golf coach, but he wasn't quite sure how, he approached the change in the same way that Blake did—by learning everything he could about the subject. He went to the leading club-fitting school in the country and he enrolled in a course. He got certified as a fitness trainer, a master club fitter, and a health coach. He worked with well-known coaches in the field and learned the art of green reading. It was from learning all these different aspects of the sport that he found his niche. There were a lot of people out there that someone could turn to if they wanted to work on their putting, for example, but not a lot of people who focused on the mental aspects of the game, on what made them play their best and what got in the way when they didn't. It was that learning journey that led Jason to become a performance coach.

The same has been true for David, who had been an avid learner throughout his career. That was true when he was first starting out and would compare his own skills and abilities against those who held the leadership positions he wanted to grow into, so he knew where to focus his efforts. It was equally true when he became CEO of a Fortune 500 company and took his team members to do "best practice" visits at some of the most successful companies in the world so they could learn what made them great. It can be true for you as well. The following exercise will get you started.

TAKE CHARGE ACTION:
Kickstart Your Learning Curve

1) Identify five things you can do to expand the pool from which you draw your insights about how you can grow yourself and reach the destination you set for yourself. These could be books you read, podcasts or TED Talks you listen to, webinars or classes you take, or interviews with someone who has been where you want to be—to name just a few options.

   For example, if you want to open a restaurant, research successful restaurateurs and find out what they have said about the business. If you are lacking skills for the promotion you want, enroll in an online class. If you're having trouble choosing an SBT, read books about goal setting or finding your purpose.

2) From each source write down takeaways that you could apply to your own situation.

3) Once you have made your way through those five things, choose five more! Learning never ends.

You have to have a good sense of who you are, but enough humility to be able to listen to others and recognize that you can always learn. When you stop learning, you cease to grow and you cease to lead.

—BONNIE HILL, cofounder of Icon Blue

Understand How Your Mind Might Not Be Helping You Succeed

To reach your destination you need insight, not just into how to move your goal forward, but also into how to tackle any roadblocks that stand in your way. If there are things in your life that are getting in the way of your joy, if it feels like you aren't growing personally or professionally in the way that you want to, if you have found you haven't been able to take steps to reach your destination—or even decide which destination is worth pursuing—there are surely reasons for that. What's getting in your way?

Everyone encounters roadblocks on their journey. There isn't a success story in the world that hasn't come with missteps, detours, and even outright failures along the way. This is exactly why it's best to prepare yourself for them ahead of time as best you can.

The roadblocks are going to be different for everyone, but no matter what you encounter, the signal that something could be getting in your way will often begin as a feeling. *I feel like a failure every time I make a sales call. I feel anxious every morning before I go to work.* In Jason's case it was: *I made this big career change that was supposed to make my life better, but I've never felt more unhappy.*

Or it may come to you as a kind of voice in your head: *I know I want to accomplish this big thing someday, but when I think about that, these sabotaging voices enter into the back of my mind.* In David's case, it might have been: *How are you ever going run a company one day if you can't give a great speech? How are you going to rise to such a position when you don't have an MBA?*

When difficult and potentially derailing thoughts or feelings enter your head, your typical reaction may be to ignore them. You might choose to push past them and keep going. Or you might find they cause you to doubt yourself and your belief in what's possible. You might even shut down entirely and stop trying. Whatever the case for you personally, consciously addressing them often isn't someone's first instinct.

There's no need to judge yourself harshly if this sounds familiar. These are common reactions, if not always productive ones. But now is the time to prepare yourself. You know that achieving your SBT won't be easy. You know the roadblocks are coming. You can accept these things as givens. Once you do that, the question becomes: What can you do now to set yourself up to manage the difficult moments that could send you off course? Before we start preparing you, let's first consider what might happen if you don't learn how to address these things.

When Jason first started working with the champion golfer Jason Day, Day was going through something that a lot of athletes go through in Jason's experience: He had lost some of his confidence. One of the reasons why Day rose to the level he was at was because his driver had always been a weapon for him. He had been able to hit long drives off the tee with better accuracy than most golfers he played against. It was something that separated him from the pack. That is, until it wasn't.

As human beings, we aren't exactly perfectly calibrated machines. Just because we can do something in a near-perfect way one day, or even most days, doesn't mean that we can do it that way the next time we try. So it shouldn't come as a big surprise that sometimes Day would step up to hit the ball and it would not go where he wanted it to go. Sometimes he would hit a bad shot.

But it did come as a surprise to Day who had come to rely on his abilities in this area. Even so, missing a shot here and there shouldn't have been a big deal in and of itself. All the pros miss sometimes, even when they're winning tournaments. The problem started when those missed shots turned into a crisis of confidence.

When he stepped up to hit the ball, instead of focusing on what he wanted to happen, Day began to focus on the *what ifs*. What if the ball went off course like it had the last time?

What if he had lost his touch? What if he couldn't rely on his driver anymore? What if he was not as good as he thought he was after all?

It became a kind of self-fulfilling prophesy for Day. The more he worried that he couldn't do it, the more shots he would miss. One of the things that Jason often says to athletes in situations like these is that the pressure they are feeling doesn't really exist outside their own minds. It's something they create themselves. It's not uncommon that the things that get in our way are actually of our own making.

Using versions of the same exercises we taught you in the last chapter, Jason worked with Day to become more *aware* of what was happening inside his head and how it was leading him astray. From there, they worked to intentionally move Day from a worried or anxious state to a more *neutral* one. Next came shifting his awareness so he could occupy his mind with more useful thoughts. In this case, that was accomplished through a process visualizing where he wanted the ball to go before he hit it. And it worked. With consistent effort, Day got his confidence back and began playing better than ever. He rose to the number-one ranking in the world after that.

Even people at the top of their games have to work on getting better, and they can always suffer setbacks. When that happens it's important to remember that our instincts don't always guide us in the right direction. There was even a point in Day's career when the pressure he was feeling caused him to want to quit the sport entirely. But he got past that feeling and went on to win tournaments. Imagine what would have happened if he had given up. Sometimes our instincts need to be disrupted for our own sake, which is why it's so important that you develop insight into what your default instincts might be.

Learn to Listen to Yourself

The clue that something in your head is getting in your way will sometimes be obvious and other times be quite subtle. It might be a quiet voice in your mind telling you that you can't, or it might be a vague feeling of anxiety. It might be the urge to turn away and not think about or talk about what's happening. It might be a sense of confusion or feeling stuck. It might be a full-blown panic attack.

The first thing to do when you pick up on one of these clues is simply to pause and accept it. Do nothing but *listen* to the voice or feeling. This can be challenging, but it's also essential to building the kind of self-knowledge we have been talking about and discovering how and when your own mind might be getting in your way.

You can use your mindset tools to help you. If you catch yourself denying or pushing past uncomfortable thoughts, practice *harnessing your awareness* by pausing and taking notice of where your focus is. Is it on the insights you could be gaining? If not, you can make a conscious effort to shift your focus in that direction rather than turning away. Use your *neutrality practices* to put you in a calmer and more open frame of mind as you do this.

It can also help to *reframe* the way we look at the challenges we will inevitably face by saying to ourselves that those uncomfortable feelings are information we can work with. We may not like them, but they are valuable in their way. They can serve as important clues about something we need to work on or resolve.

When we are aware and intentional about our thoughts and actions, it is possible to change our perspective about what's getting in our way—much like Jason Day did when he began to lose confidence in his game. We can **do this** rather than accept the roadblocks we hit or challenges we face as reasons why something can't be done. Over time, this is how we build belief in ourselves and what we are capable of.

Brian Cornell, chairman and CEO of Target, is a prime example of this. When Cornell was growing up, becoming a CEO was the furthest thing from his mind. He lost his dad when he was young and his mom struggled with her health, so he came from very humble beginnings. He spent his childhood doing things like mowing lawns, shoveling snow, and washing trucks to earn extra cash to get by. His circumstances could have been a limitation, but Brian discovered early that there were three areas in life where, as he put it, "nobody cared who my dad was or how much money I had." That was in academics, in sports, and at work. When it came to those things, it was all about how well he performed. So he said to himself, "I'm going to perform, excel, take advantage of opportunities, and somehow it all worked out."

He couldn't change where he came from, but he could change how he viewed his circumstances. Cornell chose to see opportunities, not limitations, and do what he could to take advantage of them. "If you look back in time, when I was a kid, you would have said there's no chance this person ends up doing what I'm doing." And yet he did.

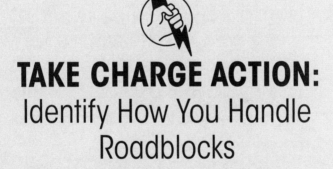

TAKE CHARGE ACTION:
Identify How You Handle Roadblocks

You can't solve a problem you cannot see, so how do you know when your own mind isn't helping you succeed? You can get some clues by looking to your past for insights. What do you typically do when something doesn't go as planned or something makes you feel uncomfortable in some way? Some typical reactions might be:

- You ignore it.
- You get anxious or worried.
- You get angry or frustrated.
- You shut down or run away.
- You find someone or something to blame.

1) Recall a situation where you hit a roadblock of some kind. Maybe it was a job or promotion you really wanted but didn't get. Maybe it was a conversation with a family member that didn't go as planned. Maybe it was a challenging circumstance or encounter that you didn't know how to handle.

2) Write down what you remember about the situation—not just the details of what happened, but also how you felt.

3) Read it over, then ask yourself: How did I respond, or not respond, when I hit this particular roadblock? (Look back at the list for inspiration.) Write that down, too.

4) Now ask yourself: Was that a typical response for me?

5) If other situations come to mind, write them down too and compare your responses. Is there a consistent pattern? Or do you react

differently in different circumstances? Don't judge how you responded. Just notice where your instincts typically lead you. Remember, the more aware you are, the more you will be able to shift your focus to where you want it to go.

6) Use this information to build your self-knowledge. When you encounter roadblocks on your journey, check to see if you are having similar reactions and whether those reactions could lead you further astray rather than helping you to solve the problem. Then use the Take Charge Actions from Chapter 2 to shift to a more productive frame of mind.

· · · · · · · · ·

TAKE CHARGE ACTION:
Listen to What Your Single Biggest Thing Is Telling You

Now that you have some insight into how you typically handle roadblocks, let's try to anticipate some of the roadblocks you might encounter on your way to reaching your destination. Write down your SBT so you can look at it as you do this exercise.

1) Read your SBT to yourself and then simply pause and listen.

2) What comes up as you think about working toward your goal? What roadblocks do you envision getting in your way? These could be internal roadblocks, like fears or anxieties that you have or sabotaging voices that might whisper in your ear. Or, they could be external roadblocks, like resources or skills you might be missing.

3) Don't try to solve any of the problems that come up. Just listen to them. And then write them down.

ADDITIONAL TACTICS TO TRY:

- If it helps to spur your thinking, you can divide your thoughts into categories. Look at each of the categories that follow and consider what comes up for you in regard to each one when you think about your destination:

- Limiting beliefs like imposter syndrome, which is a sense of inadequacy that sticks with a person even when that person succeeds[20]
- Emotional barriers like fear or anxiety
- Lack of knowledge or experience
- Blind spots or aspects of achieving your goal that you have difficulty envisioning

- If this exercise makes you uncomfortable because it feels like you are taking a close look at what you consider to be your weaknesses, then try reframing that thought. Instead of *weaknesses*, think of them as *opportunities to grow*. Growth is often uncomfortable, but the alternative—which is stagnation—doesn't feel so great either. Remember that and make an effort to look for the opportunity behind each thing you listed. In other words, don't just say, "I don't have enough experience to open a restaurant." Instead say, "I have an opportunity to learn something new and valuable that will allow me to get one step closer to my SBT."

Switch into Problem-Solving Mode

This chapter has been about collecting the insights you need to move your SBT forward. In the next chapter, we will talk about how to turn those insights into actions, but as a final word here, we want to talk about orienting your mind to do just that.

When we set out to do something new, our minds can get clouded with all the question marks and potential problems we could encounter. No one ever knows exactly how they are going to accomplish something until they do it. But when there are so many unknowns, it can cause us to become confused, disheartened, or even to shut down.

Jason once coached an executive at a tech company who was in just this sort of state. She recently had earned a promotion, and her new role meant that she had to give a keynote speech introducing a new software program her company was rolling out. She was really stressed about it because she had to give the presentation even though the software wasn't finished yet. She knew it would be ready by the time they needed to deliver it to customers, but she was going to have to wing it for her presentation. She was overwhelmed by anxiety at the prospect of the software prototype freezing while she was onstage demonstrating it. What would people think? What would she do? She just couldn't get past her negative feelings about it.

Jason didn't know anything about the work she did, but he did know something about anxiety, so when she asked him to use his performance coaching skills to help her, he agreed.

They sat down together in her conference room, and the first thing Jason said was, "Let's list all the issues you're worried about."

She started with the very first one: "The software is going to freeze." So they wrote that down. Then they continued to list about twenty more things she was nervous about, ending with, "When I walk on stage, I trip and I fall and everyone laughs at me."

After they finished the list, Jason set it aside for a moment. He guided the executive through some breathing exercises and a five-minute meditation. By then she appeared to be in a calm and neutral state.

So they went back to the list. He said to her, "Okay, now imagine that you have a magic lamp. You're going to rub it and a genie is going to come out who will tell you the solution to the first problem. What would that solution be?"

Without missing a beat, the executive said, "How about I just do a PowerPoint presentation with screenshots of the software. I can click through the screens that I need people to see, and they won't even know that the software isn't running live."

Jason thought that was a great solution, so they wrote it down. They continued through the list like that, one after the other, until they got to the last one—the prospect of her trip-ping and falling. She decided that she could wear flat shoes and have a joke ready to laugh it off in case it actually hap-pened, even though her nervousness had subsided enough by then that she realized it probably wouldn't. And that was it. In maybe an hour's time, she created all these solutions where she had seen only problems before. It was a shift in mindset, from seeing problems to looking for solutions, that made the difference—because she had obviously known the answers all along. What's more, the process of finding those solutions helped ease the fears and anxieties she was having about getting on stage for her first big presentation in her new role.

So, as you move on to the next chapter, which is all about taking productive action toward reaching your destination, remember this problem-solving mindset and make an effort to channel it.

4

The Self-Coaching Journey

Take Insightful Action

• • • • • • • •

Your Self-Coaching Journey Toolkit

 Turn Insight into Action

 Start Your Roadmap

 Track Your Progress

 Appreciate Yourself

 Flip the Script

eAC

Life is like riding a bicycle. To keep your balance you must keep moving.

—ALBERT EINSTEIN, in a letter to his son[21]

You have uncovered some insights. Now what can you do about them?

It's no accident that the last chapter included a humility-building exercise. If you want to move forward in a productive way, it helps to admit something humbling, which is that none of us knows exactly what we should do to become the people we want to be or reach the destinations we want to reach. After all, every time we set a new objective, we're treading new territory. The path to achieving something new will always be a question mark until we walk it. So what do we do with that question mark? We can start by admitting we won't have all the answers up front and we don't need to. It's not a reason to get stuck or hold ourselves back. Instead we can take action to move ourselves forward, step by step, in spite of not having all the answers.

But that doesn't mean taking action for action's sake. It's an important distinction. We want to take *insightful* actions; that is, actions that are both informed and inspired.

As you take action toward achieving your Single Biggest Thing, strive for a balance between the two: information and inspiration. That balance is about keeping your feet on the ground and your head in the clouds at the same time. It's about having enough grounding to see the reality of where you are now, while also having enough inspiration to imagine the possibilities of where you could go tomorrow. You can't achieve anything new unless you have some of both.

The dangers of becoming unbalanced and falling too far to one side or another are these:

- If you're too focused on your present reality, then you could get stuck and hold yourself back from growing in new and unexpected directions.
- On the flip side, if your view of your potential is too pie-in-the-sky and not anchored in reality, then you could set yourself up for failure.

Jason once coached a teenager whose goal was to become a pro golfer one day, and this was no pie-in-the-sky goal. The kid had a real shot. He was one of the best junior golfers in the world at the time.

One day Jason picked up the young golfer for a coaching session. As they were driving to the course, out of nowhere the kid just started crying. So naturally Jason asked him what was going on.

"My mom's really on my case," he said.

"About what?" Jason asked, thinking the answer would be something about household chores or not getting his homework done.

"About my proximity to the hole at 150 yards," the kid responded. "It's only like 25 feet. She says I can't make enough birdies if I keep hitting the ball to only 25 feet."

It was clear to Jason that this young athlete needed some encouragement and inspiration, as well as a healthy dose of reality. So he gave him his phone and said: "Do me a favor. Go to the PGA Tour website and look up what the average proximity to the hole stats are for PGA Tour players."

He did as Jason asked and discovered the answer was about 27 feet from 150 yards. The kid's average was about 25 feet. He was barely a teenager, and he was already doing better than the average adult tour player when it came to this aspect of the game.

The reality was that the kid's expectations (or, more accurately, his mom's) were out of whack, and it was making him really upset about a game he usually loved to play. That one piece of data changed his perspective, giving him both a more realistic picture of his accomplishments and greater inspiration for what he might be able to achieve one day. And that balanced perspective is what allowed him to move forward with his training in a positive way.

In this chapter, we're going to make use of the insights you have gained to take action and move you forward. As you do this, remember to try to maintain that balance to help you stay on track.

Turn Insight into Action

That junior golfer was able to gain valuable perspective about his game and his chances of achieving his SBT, which was to turn pro one day. But that kind of insight can do more than just provide perspective; it can also provide a path forward.

The young golfer's proximity to the hole average was in good shape when he looked at it in context, but what about his other stats? How did his putting average compare to professional players? What about his average driver distance? The destination he was aiming for was the PGA, so a useful path forward could be to compare himself to the pros in as many areas as he could find statistics for. That would show him where to focus his efforts in order to improve his game. You can apply that same way of thinking to reach your SBT.

That's what David did when it came to his desire to run something someday. He knew that one of the things that could stand in his way was his discomfort with public speaking. He had gathered insights by paying attention to leaders in positions he aspired to, and the ones he admired most were able to stand in front of groups of people and really motivate them. He knew it would be a huge competitive advantage if he could rise to that level, but for years he felt like he was floundering in this area. Some moments had even been cringeworthy.

Early in his career, during his first big presentation, he had been so nervous that he had said "you know" practically once per sentence. He remembers going home afterward and burying his head in his pillow. Then, there was his first big end of the year meeting when he was head of the Frito-Lay account for the advertising agency where he worked. It was the agency's largest account, so it was an important presentation. Unfortunately, his stage fright caused him to give such a wooden and uncomfortable performance that he basically blocked it out afterward. When he was running marketing for Pizza Hut, he had to present his annual operating plan to all the top brass. He brought a box containing his speech notes to the podium, and as he set it down, he immediately knocked over several glasses of water. The mic was on so everyone could hear the clatter. "I'm either very nervous or I've wet my pants," he said to the waiting crowd.

That feeling that he was failing in this area stuck with David for years, even as he rose in his career to positions of greater and greater authority. It was something that just wasn't going away on its own, no matter how much he wanted it to. So he finally set a goal for himself of becoming a great public speaker, and to get there he decided to work with a speech coach.

David was at PepsiCo at the time, so he used one of the tactics we talked about in the last chapter: He asked someone he respected for insight about what he could do. In this case, he went to the head of HR. That person referred him to a communications expert named Jim McAlinden, who had worked with many executives at PepsiCo. When David met him for the first time, he described how painful it was for him to speak, how he worried about making mistakes, and how his past experiences left him feeling anxious about doing it again. But he also told McAlinden he wanted to get past all that because he really felt like he had potential. After all, he thought he was often pretty good after five or ten minutes, once he got past his nerves. But for all his efforts, he just wasn't improving the way he wanted to.

McAlinden helped turn his insights into action steps he could take to improve his performance. First, he showed David how to revise his speech so the sentences were shorter, making them more impactful and easier to remember. Next, he showed David examples of top-notch speakers and had him pay attention to their gestures, modulations of tone, and use of the stage. He also taught David different tactics like how to use long pauses for effect. Finally, he had David practice a speech he planned to give at the Dallas Convention Center in front of a nerve-wracking 6,000 people. McAlinden videotaped David and had him watch himself, comparing each aspect of his own performance to the successful speakers he'd just seen. David saw the difference right away.

By breaking things down in this way, not only did David have some specific things he could practice to make himself better, but he also had tangible things to focus on other than his nerves. The process made it easier for him to focus on his audience, whom he wanted to connect with, rather than on himself and how he was coming across. That shift in focus led to a new reality.

David was scheduled to be the closing speaker that evening in Dallas, and it had been a hard day for the massive crowd of Pepsi employees in attendance. The company was in a slump at the time, and most of the speakers who came before him had talked about how the company was failing expectations in one area or another. It had been a tough pill to swallow.

David had long understood the value of balancing information and inspiration. The crowd had already received a healthy dose of reality, so it was time for something different. When David got up on stage after so much bad news, he started off by using one of those long pauses McAlinden had taught him. He stood there, looking out at the crowd and saying nothing for a few seconds. The crowd had grown quiet in anticipation by the time he opened with: "There's one thing I want you all to know: This is one great company, and I don't want anyone here to forget it."

It was like he'd shaken up a bottle of Pepsi before unscrewing the top. The crowd exploded.

Then, something spontaneously started to catch on with the audience. David said something, and some members of the audience called out "uh huh." Then he said something else, and a few more responded with "uh huh." This was back when a series of popular commercials for Diet Pepsi were airing featuring Ray Charles singing "You Got the Right

One Baby, Uh Huh." Pretty soon the entire crowd of 6,000 was engaged in this kind of call-and-response. It changed the spirit of the entire conference, and it ended up being one of the best speeches of David's career.

What's even better is that the moment helped David really turn a corner. It unlocked his ability to free himself up and be himself when he speaks. Now he *loves* giving speeches. He can't wait to get in front of people. It's a talent and skill that has served him well ever since. It's also proof that small steps can lead to real, lasting, big changes.

TAKE CHARGE ACTION:
Turn Insight into Action

To create a path forward, we're going to start with a bit of brainstorming.

1) Gather together all the insights you gained in the last chapter. It could be from your research or from talking to others, ideas you came up with on your own about what you might need to do and what might stand in your way, anything.

2) Next, start turning those insights into actions, meaning things you can *do* to start moving closer to your SBT. For example, if you are looking to create your own podcast, someone you talked to might have recommended some great ones to listen to for inspiration, or passed along contact info for their producers. So you might write down "listen to podcasts" and "contact producers" as action steps. You might also write down things you thought of yourself like "research methods for marketing podcasts and connecting with listeners."

3) Make a list of all the actions you can think of. Each of these things is a potential step along your journey. We'll call these your *goals*. Don't worry about the how or the when just yet. Simply write them down as if you're creating a long to-do list.

4) Look at your list and determine if any of the goals can be broken down further into smaller goals or action steps. For example, when David set his sights on running a division or company, he might have written down "become a better public speaker" as a goal to help him get there. But that's a pretty big

goal. His speech coach helped him break
that down even further into steps like:

   a. Research speakers you admire and
      watch their performances.

   b. Analyze what you respond to about
      those performances.

   c. Record yourself giving a speech.

   d. Watch it and compare your perfor-
      mance to the speakers you admire.

5) Hold on to your list. We'll continue working with
it in the next Take Charge Action.

SELF-COACHING TIP: Brainstorm as many possible actions as you can, but avoid the trap of feeling like your list has to be perfect or complete. Journeys to new destinations never start off with perfectly complete roadmaps. You will find your way there as you go.

Define Your Current Reality

By now you know where you want to go—your SBT. You just defined some of the steps you will need to take to get there.

Before you start plotting your journey, let's make sure you have a clear view of where you're starting from—your current reality.

David once coached a young man named Ralph, whose SBT was to become an entrepreneur. However, when David starting coaching him, he was working as a junior person at one of the major financial companies. When he first applied for that job, he wanted desperately to get it because it allowed him to analyze a lot of different companies and learn business from the ground up. But the reality of the job wasn't as exciting as he'd hoped. He was working eighty hours a week, and a lot of that time was spent doing things he didn't really enjoy. As a result, he was frustrated and ready to leave the company for something else.

Before he did that, David helped him adopt a clear, unbiased view of his current situation. Was he ready to be an entrepreneur? Probably not. He hadn't yet learned enough about how to start a business or run a company. Did he have the funds to support himself while he figured it out? Not really. This realistic perspective helped Ralph make a decision that would help him get closer to his SBT, even if he wasn't ready to make a huge leap yet.

We started this book by asking what brings you joy. We believe it's essential to keep an eye trained on your joy while you make decisions about what you want to do and where you want to go in life. Does that mean that every single thing you do will be joyful? Of course not.

Ralph wasn't feeling a lot of joy in his current position. But would he feel joy if he left it and found himself broke and struggling while he tried to become the entrepreneur he wasn't yet ready to be? That was unlikely. David reminded him that the reason he had wanted the job in the first place was to have an opportunity to learn. Was he learning? Yes, he said he was learning a lot.

David helped Ralph accept the reality of his situation. While he wasn't doing exactly what he wanted to do right now, he was learning things that would help him get where he wanted to go. David said to him, "You can become an entrepreneur if that's what you want, but right now why not focus on making sure you'll be a good one when you get there?"

The reality was that Ralph needed more experience before he could achieve his SBT. It was similar to the situation David once found himself in when he took a job in operations—a role he'd never imagined himself in before—in order to show people he could be more than just a marketing guy. Some steps on your path will be more joyful than others, but doing big things takes hard work and sometimes requires trade-offs. Or, as David said to Ralph, "Sometimes you have to eat some cold eggs on the way to getting the really hot ones with the bacon and toast."

TAKE CHARGE ACTION:
Start Your Roadmap

Approach your SBT in the same way that you would think about training for a marathon. (Maybe running a marathon is actually your SBT!) You wouldn't go from sitting on the couch to running 26-plus miles in one day. You'd start by considering the reality of where you are right now: How far am I able to run right now? Can I even run at all?

Then you would use the answers to those questions as your starting place and set a series of smaller goals to work your way up to a marathon-length run. You might start with the first mile or half mile, or even a walk around the block, if that's what you need to do.

When you know where you are and you know where you want to go (that's your SBT), then the task becomes about plotting the route from here and there. Use the following steps to get started.

1) At the top of a blank page, write down where you are now. Make an effort to paint a real,

unbiased picture. For example, if your goal is to start a restaurant, you might write at the top of your page something like: "I know a lot about food and restaurants, having worked in them since I was a teenager. I have a somewhat clear vision of what I want the restaurant to be. But I know I will need money to start it, and I am currently $50,000 in debt with a below-average credit score."

2) At the bottom of the page, write down your SBT.

3) Your task now is to start plotting the route from here to there. In the last exercise, you came up with a list of goals. These are some of the steps you will need to take to achieve your SBT. We are going to work on prioritizing those goals now. Look at your list and ask yourself: Do some goals need to be achieved before others? Put a star next to those or reorder your list accordingly.

4) Are some goals questionable? Maybe someone suggested you try something or contact someone, but you're unsure how useful it would be. Put a question mark next to anything like that.

5) Pick a starting place. You don't have to over-think this. We suggest you avoid the question mark goals for now, and start with something that's not overwhelming but that could really be useful. Ask yourself: What's one thing I could start doing today? Write that down as your first step and make a plan for when and how you will get it done.

6) When you accomplish that, where do you think it will lead? What could you do next? And then next after that? Start filling in the space between your current reality at the top of the page and your SBT at the bottom.

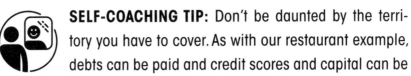 **SELF-COACHING TIP:** Don't be daunted by the territory you have to cover. As with our restaurant example, debts can be paid and credit scores and capital can be raised. Get into a neutral frame of mind and look with clear eyes at the territory you need to cover to get from one place to the other. Then remind yourself that you don't need to cover it all at once, just one step at a time.

Bring Your Focus Down to What to Do Next

Setting an SBT can be overwhelming. Your list of goals and the roadmap you have begun to create may feel long, incomplete, and even messy at this point. There may be a lot of knowledge you need to gain, skills you have to develop, experiences you need to have, and benchmarks you need to hit before you can get there. And that's just the things you know about. There are also unknown obstacles that will come up along the way, as we talked about in Chapter 3.

If you try to think about all the things you have to do all at once, it can lead to confusion, distress, or even cause a shutdown because there's just too much to consider. A more effective approach is to simply focus on the process. You have a general (if sketchy or incomplete) roadmap on how to get where you want to go. Now focus on the next step you need to take to move closer to your destination. There's an old adage that's worth keeping in mind here: Dream big, but start small. Or, as the ancient philosopher Lao Tzu famously put it, "The journey of a thousand miles begins with a single step."

For example, say your goal is to grow your business by 20%. If you did the last exercise, then you will have broken that down into things you think are necessary to achieve that. Your task now is to simply focus on them one at a time. You might be wondering if your sales staff is big enough to handle that increase in volume. Well, don't just wonder. Focus on doing that analysis. Once that's complete, focus on hiring the people you need to boost sales. Then focus on making sure those new hires get up to speed quickly so they can start selling. Then focus on the next thing after that. One thing at a time, over and over again, is how you make progress.

David once interviewed serial entrepreneur Jessica Kim, who talked about the very first business she ever started in college, a baking business that she ran out of her dorm room at Brown University. She called it Jessica's Wonders, and it began one day when she walked into a local pizzeria and saw a plate of banana bread for sale. It was nothing fancy, just pieces of bread in Saran wrap with a toothpick sticking out advertising the price. She looked at that and thought, "I can do better than this." The next day she brought in some of her own special banana bread and asked the owner if he would consider trying to sell it. He agreed, and she sold out in a day. So she kept making it, and the pizzeria kept selling it. Pretty soon she expanded to thirteen different hotspots around campus, and she was on her way to building a viable business.

From there she expanded into supermarkets, but Kim had a steep learning curve along the way. She was a good home baker, but she had no professional training. Once she started getting more and more orders, she realized she had no idea how to make her recipes in bulk. She didn't know what to do, so she turned to another local business for help. One day she walked into a nearby bagel shop and asked the owner if he could give her some advice. And he did. He

invited her to come to the shop at 4:00 a.m. the next morning when he started baking, and he showed her what she
needed to know to turn out her recipes in larger quantities.

Perhaps it was because the business grew organically that
Kim never got too ahead of herself. She learned what to do
along the way, focusing on the next problem that needed
to be solved or the next way she might be able to grow her
business. When she found herself in that spot of not knowing what to do next, she explained, "What I did was look for
someone that knew just a bit more than me ... We often think
we need this famous expert or the best mentor in the world
in order to move forward, but you just need to find someone
that knows a bit more."

This perspective can help keep you from becoming overwhelmed or unfocused. It's great if you have a clear and full
step by step vision for how you're going to accomplish something (as long as you keep an open and flexible coaching
mindset in case something doesn't go according to plan),
but it isn't necessary to achieve success. The late Colin Powell once characterized his work as National Security Advisor
and then Chairman of the Joint Chiefs of Staff as a process
of "constant decision-making." As a result, he developed a
philosophy about decision-making that he described simply as this: "Dig up all the information you can, then go with
your instincts."[22] He even boiled that down into what became
known as his 40/70 Rule, which says that you don't have to
wait until you're 100% sure before you get started. If you did,

TAKE CHARGE OF YOU

I don't think I had one singular thing that changed my life overnight. I mentor a lot of people ... about the restaurant business, and I tell them, I'm still not a success story. Like, I still grind it every day. My climb to success was slow and gradual. It was bit by bit. And I appreciate that.

—EDWARD LEE, chef and restaurateur

---

it would often be too late. Instead do your homework, get somewhere between 40% and 70% of the information you need, and then act and see what happens.

Of course this rule didn't even lead Colin Powell to choose the right actions every time, but over the course of his career, he did manage to do some pretty good things and get pretty far. None of us can ever be 100% right in the actions we choose, but we can bank on the fact that if we get stuck in uncertainty and don't even try, then it's 100% certain that we won't get very far at all. So remember your humility and your open coaching mindset. You won't know exactly what works or how well it will work until you start. So you just need to start. Just move the ball forward. And then do it again. And then again and again after that.

Track Your Progress

As a performance coach, Jason tracks the progress of every one of the athletes he works with. He does that by grading the quality of every single shot they take. He does that by timing how long their pre-shot routine takes and watching how they shift their vision (which indicates to him whether they are taking the time to visualize where they want the ball to go before they hit it), and comparing those things to how successful the shot is in reaching its target.

As a self-coach, you're going to have to track progress for yourself. The process is going to be different depending on the kind of destination you're aiming for, but it's crucial for two very important reasons:

1) Tracking progress shows you what's working and what isn't so you can course correct or take more effective actions in the future.

2) Tracking progress provides inspiration and motivation because when you can see yourself making progress, it makes your far-away destination feel more real and attainable.

In these two ways, the act of tracking your progress accomplishes both the things this chapter is set up to do: It provides you with information you can use to continue your progress and the inspiration to keep going.

Years ago, before he had a hit television show, Jerry Seinfeld tracked his own progress toward becoming a successful comedian. He knew the way to become a better comic was to write better jokes, and the way to write better jokes was to write more often. So he created a system to put pressure on himself to do just that. It started with a giant wall calendar that showed an entire year on one page. He hung it in a place where he couldn't help but see it often. Then he got himself a big red marker. He told himself that he would write a certain amount every day, and every time he did that, he would make a big red X on the calendar for that day to indicate that he'd succeeded.

"After a few days you'll have a chain," he once explained. "Just keep at it and the chain will grow longer every day. You'll like seeing that chain, especially when you get a few weeks under your belt. Your only job next is to not break the chain. Don't break the chain!"[23]

TAKE CHARGE ACTION:
Track Your Progress

How you track your progress will depend on the destination you have set for yourself. Use the roadmap you have created to help you. It may be a work in progress, but it can also be seen as a long to-do list that you can use to track your journey. The following tips will also help:

1) Write things down: Research shows that a person is more likely to achieve a goal that he or she has written down. So don't keep your to-dos trapped in your head!

2) Check things off: Take inspiration from Jerry Seinfeld and make a big X or check mark when you have accomplished something. Remember, when you see the progress you're making, it will inspire you to keep going.

3) Quantify what you can: If your SBT is to get promoted, then you might just have a checklist of things to do like: 1) learn new skills, 2) make contacts with relevant people, 3) talk to your boss about your intentions, and so on. You can check off things like that as you accomplish them. But sometimes you can put numbers to your progress, which makes things easier to track. If you need a certain amount of money to start a new business, how much do you need to save each month? If you're losing weight, how many pounds should you shed each week? If you're aiming to increase sales, how many more products need to be sold each quarter, month, or week? Break down the numbers into small, manageable goals when you can.

4) Set a timeframe: Again, this will be easier and more straightforward for some goals than for others. For example, if you want to get promoted, the timeframe isn't entirely up to you, but you could say something like, "Get promoted within three years or start looking for new opportunities." If you want to lose weight in order to achieve the SBT of improving your overall health, however, that's easier to quantify and put a timeframe around: "Lose twenty pounds in three months."

You can't worry about [playing on] Sunday because you can't be effective on Sunday if you don't take care of Monday. And so every single day, I'm just staying completely in the moment. I'm being the best Larry Fitzgerald on Monday, I'll be the best Larry Fitzgerald on Tuesday, I'll be the best Larry Fitzgerald on Wednesday, and if I'm doing that every single day, why would I not be the best on Sunday when I step out on that field? And I think when I step on the field it gives me unbelievable confidence knowing that I did all the work already.

—LARRY FITZGERALD, retired NFL wide receiver

Learn How to Talk to Yourself

Inspiration is essential to helping you sustain yourself on what could be a long and challenging journey, which is why it's important to keep in mind how easily inspiration can be undercut. This is especially true when you're entering new territory and trying to achieve big things. That's why it's important to be conscious of how we talk to ourselves about what we want to do and our efforts to be successful. We can send ourselves off course more easily than many of us realize.

Remember in Chapter 2 when we talked about negativity bias (the idea that humans are hardwired to emphasize the negative over the positive)? Research shows that negative words and experiences stick in our minds and have a greater psychological effect than positive ones. This may sound like a bit of a bummer, but it's just the reality of how the human brain works. Of course, when we're conscious of that fact, we can work with the reality and find productive ways to address and move past it.

To do that, we can focus on building even more self-awareness by tuning in to how we talk to ourselves about what we want to achieve and our ability to achieve it. Do we beat ourselves up when we make a mistake or fail to anticipate something that gets in our way? Do we tell ourselves things that will damage our inspiration and motivation, like we can't do it, or we're not good enough, or no one will take

TAKE CHARGE OF YOU

us seriously? It's not difficult to do some real damage to our belief in ourselves if we don't learn to manage those negative voices in our heads.

Before Jason became a performance coach, when he was still figuring out what his next career should be, he and his wife went to see a movie called *Slumdog Millionaire*. If you haven't seen it, it's about a kid in India who loses contact with his childhood love. But he never gives up on her, going to extraordinary lengths to find her again, including becoming a contestant on *Who Wants to Be a Millionaire?* because he knows she watches the show. Jason and his wife saw the movie on New Year's Eve, and he walked out of the theater inspired to make a New Year's resolution: to never make a decision based in fear again.

The very next day, on New Year's Day, Jason and his wife, Elizabeth, were talking about what he wanted to do next in his career. She had been there for him when he left his job at the boat company, and then again when he started feeling like he'd made a mistake by starting a new career in real estate. Since it was a new year and a time of new beginnings, Elizabeth thought she'd make a suggestion: "You love golf," she said to Jason. "Why don't you consider a career in golf?"

"I do love it," he admitted, "but I was never a professional golfer. I never even played college golf. So why would anyone ever listen to me?"

Without missing a beat, Elizabeth looked at him and said, "That sounds like a decision based in fear."

That was the beginning of Jason's journey to becoming a performance coach. But if it hadn't been for Elizabeth, Jason could have talked himself out of the career that has brought him so much joy and aligns perfectly with his values and purpose. It's invaluable to have those people in our lives who can catch us when our negative self-talk is getting in our way, but it's also something we need to learn to do for ourselves. The following Take Charge Actions can help.

TAKE CHARGE ACTION:
Appreciate Yourself

This exercise will help you shift your self-talk to a more positive place. David has used it for years when giving feedback to team members, but it works equally well if you apply it to yourself.

We all have weakness. We all make mistakes. There are always things that any one of us could do to improve ourselves or make improvements in our work. But saying to someone, "You messed this up" or "You could have done this better" isn't a particularly motivating—or effective—way to boost performance.

If it doesn't work well to talk to other people this way, why would it work to talk this way to yourself? When you're tracking your progress and analyzing what's working for you and what's not, pay attention to how to talk to yourself. Use the following steps to do it in a more effective way by putting yourself in a more positive and productive frame of mind.

1) Focus first on what works: What do you appreciate most about your efforts? What has worked the best?

2) Write those things down and then ask yourself this question: How could you be even more effective?

3) Avoid the word *but*. Don't say: "You did this one thing really well, *but* you didn't do this other thing that you should have." Instead say: "You did this one thing really well, *and* you could be even better if you did this other thing as well."

TAKE CHARGE ACTION:
Flip the Script

When you hear a voice in your head that causes you to doubt your ability, that means it's a good time to pause and be curious. Remember that the coaching mindset asks us to stay open to whatever is going to move us forward, so rather than believing or denying the voice, be curious. Use that curiosity as a starting point for a conversation and ask yourself some questions:

1) What if it's not true?
2) What are you feeling about the situation and why?
3) What are the facts about the situation?
4) What options do you have now versus what you originally thought?

Let's play that out by returning to our example of the junior golfer who was told by his mom that he would never be able to make enough birdies to win if he didn't improve his proximity to the hole average from 150 yards.

First, he could have asked himself what would happen if that piece of information he had been given wasn't true. If it was untrue, then he wouldn't have to worry so much about the chances of achieving his dream of playing professionally. It's important to ask yourself this question because it gets you to start thinking differently. It puts you in a frame of mind to analyze the merits of what you're being told versus accepting it without question.

Second, he could have realized that the situation was causing him to doubt himself and feel like he wasn't measuring up. Those kinds of feelings were not going to contribute to his success, so he would need to find a way to return to a neutral state or reframe the situation.

Third, he did find out with Jason's help that the facts of the matter didn't support what he was being told. He was in fact better than the average pro golfer when it came to this particular stat, and he hadn't even gone pro yet!

Fourth and finally, that process opened up a world of options for him. He could work toward improving his stat in that area. Or he could work on other aspects of his game where he was actually lagging behind professional players. Most importantly, he could realize that what he was already doing was working pretty well for him, and he could keep going without being held back by doubts or bad information.

That's one of the most important things you need to be able to do in order to achieve just about anything in life: You need to be able to keep going. It's so important, in fact, that we have devoted the next and final chapter to setting yourself up to do just that.

5

The Self-Coaching Habit

Commit to Constant Improvement

· · · · · · · ·

Your Self-Coaching Habit Toolkit

 Build Your Motivational Space

 Choose How You Want to Feel Today

 Share Your Intention

 Create Your Personal Highlight Reel

 Raise the Bar Year after Year

Success is not final; failure is not fatal. It is the courage to continue that counts.

—WINSTON CHURCHILL

No process is worth very much if it isn't sustainable, which brings us to this final chapter. To wrap up the book, we're going to talk about how you can keep yourself motivated, on track, and moving forward as you continue to coach yourself to your Single Biggest Thing, and then on to greater and greater heights.

It is making a consistent effort that so often makes the difference in our success. Harry Arnett, cofounder of Municipal, a new sports utility clothing company, talked about a ritual he does every day before he goes to work. "Every morning before I leave, I tell my kids, my wife, let's go make sure we have a better day today than we did yesterday, and let's have a positive influence on at least one person today. And I tell myself that before I even get out of the car."

It was this approach that helped him get through a difficult turnaround period at a previous company he worked at when they were going through a lot of growing pains. "I always recognized that my role as the leader [was] to be this positive force of positive energy for the people that I encountered and for the company." Sometimes that would even mean staying outside in the parking lot in his car in the morning until he felt ready to show up that way. That's how committed he was to having a positive influence on people. Every. Single. Day.

The late Jack Welch, former CEO of General Electric, used to call this "the relentless drumbeat for performance." Jamie Dimon, CEO of JPMorgan Chase, likes to say that "first-rate execution beats first-rate strategy with second-rate execution." This is a concept that every truly successful person we know has come to understand—that even the best-conceived ideas, dreams, goals, plans, and strategies mean very little if you don't follow through on them.

This is true for the SBT you have set for yourself, as well as for your personal development as a whole. There is always progress to be made. It's a continual process that lasts throughout your entire career—your entire life, really. In this chapter, we will work to embrace that idea and set you up to make the most of it.

Build in Positive Motivation

Too many people leave their motivation up to chance. They wake up in the morning, think about how they're feeling, and act accordingly. But guess what? If you do that, there are going to be days when you just don't *feel* like it—whatever that *it* is to you in that moment. Ask anyone who has fallen short or gotten off track when it comes to an exercise regimen or diet plan. Leaving your motivation up to chance guarantees there will be times when you don't follow through.

That's because motivation doesn't just happen. Contrary to popular belief, it isn't something you just wake up and will yourself to have. If you have trouble staying motivated from time to time, that doesn't make you weak; it makes you human. If you want to stay motivated, it works best if you build that motivation into your process. That way you can't help but feel motivated to keep pursuing your SBT, even when things get tough or when your energy or belief wanes.

What follows are three strategies to put in place *before* you need them to help sustain your motivation. Don't wait until you have a bad day or a setback to do these. Do them now so that when the rough patches come—and they will come—you have strategies in place to turn to.

Strategy 1: Remind Yourself What Matters

It can be really easy to get caught up in the day-to-day minutia of what we need to do and where we need to go, thereby losing track of big-picture things like our SBT, our purpose, and the values that really matter to us. That's why, wherever and whenever possible, we believe it's important to surround ourselves with reminders of these things.

David does this by being intentional about what he surrounds himself with on a daily basis. His Yum! Brands office has pictures of people whose contributions to the company he has recognized over the years—so many of them, in fact, that when the walls filled up, he started using the space on the ceiling. Similarly, his entire home office has become a reminder of what's important to him and a motivational space. He has awards he has won. He has framed some of the speeches he's most proud of and has pictures of his family: his parents, his wife, Wendy, and his daughter, Ashley.

When Ashley was born, she was ten weeks premature and ended up in the NICU. The doctor told David and Wendy that she could have brain damage, heart damage, all sorts of terrible things. He talked about respiratory distress syndrome, the condition that had tragically killed Jackie and John F. Kennedy's newborn son after he had been born prematurely. In terms of a prognosis, he offered little more than "we will just have to wait and see."

When David went to the NICU to see Ashley for the first time, Wendy was still in intensive care so he went alone. After everything the doctor had told them, it was difficult not to be frightened by all the IVs she had sticking out of her tiny frame, and her skin color, which was bright red because of the drugs she was on. But when David saw her, he thought she looked so beautiful and he instinctively reached down and put his finger in her hand. Despite how weak she was, her little hand grabbed onto his finger and held it.

When David felt Ashley grab his finger, he just knew she was going to live. He hung on to that and never wavered through the tough days to come. It was another three

TAKE CHARGE OF YOU

weeks before they could bring her home from the hospital, still so small they had to dress her in doll clothes. But she was healthy. And she has been ever since. David has a picture of that moment—of her tiny hand holding on to his finger—on the wall in his office, followed by dozens more of her growing up, graduating from school and college, getting married, and now with her own three kids by her side. The images travel all the way around his office like a timeline of her life.

Those pictures, along with everything else he has on display, have essentially turned his office into a shrine to what keeps him going—the things that matter most, inspire him, and make him want to do and be better every single day. David picked up this tactic from his dad, Charles. When Charles retired from his job as a government surveyor, he was given three gifts that meant a lot to him. Some people might stick those things in a closet or drawer, but not Charles. "I'm going to put these in my 'I love me' corner," he said. Everybody should aspire to have such a corner somewhere in their home or office to serve as a reminder of what keeps them going day after day.

Jason does something similar, with posters, tournament flags, and photos all around his house as grateful reminders of the people he's gotten a chance to help through his coaching over the years and of the fact that he gets to live his purpose to serve others every day.

TAKE CHARGE ACTION:
Build Your Motivational Space

1) Pick a spot that you look at often. It could be in your office, near your computer monitor. It could be at home, in a corner of your bedroom or living room. It could be on your refrigerator. It could be anywhere that works for you. Wherever it is, make sure to place there a card with your SBT written on it, as well as ones with your purpose and values. That will keep these things top of mind and underscore their importance.

2) While you're at it, place there anything else that will remind you of why you work so hard to accomplish the things you want to accomplish and be the person you want to be. These could be pictures, awards, notes of thanks from colleagues, really anything that holds meaning for you.

3) Visit this place often, and not just on difficult days when your motivation needs a boost.

Strategy 2: Connect with Your Future Vision

Remember at the end of the very first chapter in this book, when we asked you to paint a picture for yourself of what it would mean to accomplish your SBT. The goal was for you to visualize what your future would look like if your SBT happened and to imagine how it would make you feel.

Revisit that exercise now and remind yourself of what you wrote (or drew or made into a collage, if that's what you chose to do). Pay particular attention to what you think it will *feel* like to succeed. Then ask yourself how you can bring a bit of that feeling into your life on a daily basis.

Jason once made a suggestion like this to his client, Meghan Klingenberg, professional soccer player for the Portland Thorns and World Cup champion. Klingenberg has long kept a soccer journal, a notebook where she writes down what she wants to work on, plans her daily training, and keeps track of what has been going well and what she wants to get better at. When she told Jason about her journal, he pointed out that a lot of the goals she would set for herself were outcome-oriented, meaning they were based on things like how well she played, how well her team played, and whether they won or lost. Of course someone at her level wants to win, but it's important to remember that outcomes aren't entirely up to us. This becomes especially obvious in a team sport where you can play your very best one day and still walk away from the game with a loss. But in reality, it's true for all of us. There is only so much of our lives that are within our control. So how do we keep ourselves motivated in spite of that?

Jason suggested to Klingenberg that she set a daily intention for herself that followed two rules: 1) it was not outcome-oriented, and 2) it had to be within her control. Klingenberg's intention can change from day to day—sometimes it's to "play like a kid," while other times it's to "radiate joy" or to really "connect with people"—but regardless of what she chooses, the practice has made a real difference, and not just for her. After she started doing this on a regular basis, she had a meeting with her coach who told her, completely unprompted, that a number of her teammates had recently credited her with helping them feel more connected and accepted among the team—and they were playing better as a result. With all the success she has had in her career, she considered that, far and away, one of the best compliments she ever received.

Despite the fact that our culture tends to prioritize our logical side over our emotional one, it is our *feelings* that tend to motivate us more often than facts. David, for example, believes that it was his pursuit of joy that guided him through his entire career, from advertising copywriter all the way to CEO. And because he has worked with Jason on his game, he now uses this idea when he plays golf, too. Because he would so often get down on himself when he wasn't doing well, he decided to set an intention of having more fun while he played. He had to remind himself of that recently when, during a windy day on the course, he got off to a terrible start on the first nine holes. But then he remembered his intention, telling himself that it was just a round of golf and he could still choose to enjoy the rest of the round. That change in attitude created a change in his game, and he actually shot four under par on the back nine—the first time in his life that he'd ever done so!

So pay attention to your feelings, and make an effort to be more intentional about cultivating the positive ones that will keep you motivated over the long term.

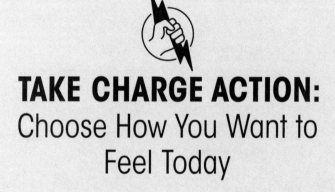

TAKE CHARGE ACTION:
Choose How You Want to Feel Today

1) First thing in the morning, ask yourself: "How do I want to feel today?" Maybe the answer is similar to some of the feelings we have already talked about—joyful, playful, connected, grateful—or something else that comes to mind.

2) Set an intention to bring that feeling into your day as much as possible. To get you started, ask yourself: What's one thing I can do today to feel this way?

3) Make an effort to do that one thing. And then do another and another after that. Keep coming back to your intention throughout the day, and look for ways to cultivate that feeling.

4) Make this a daily practice, every morning, and see what happens.

Strategy 3: Go Public

David has long used this tactic, for goals large and small, to make them feel more urgent and keep them top of mind. He goes public by telling people what he wants to do and asking them to hold him accountable for doing it.

For example, a number of years back, he decided he wanted to lose about forty pounds, so he enlisted in a weight-loss and exercise program. He was CEO of Yum! Brands at the time, and he told everyone around him what he was doing. He even offered the same program he was on to anyone else in the office who wanted to take it. It became a shared experience and a regular part of daily conversation with the people he worked with. When he began to lose weight, people could see it and would talk with him about it. And it worked. He established healthy eating and workout habits and reached his weight goal. It was good timing too because, not long after, he received his cancer diagnosis. He credits the fact that he was in such good shape when it happened for helping him get through his treatment.

It changes our thinking when we know someone is watching our progress. And when our belief or energy wanes, drawing on others can help us get it back. That's what happened to Jason when he wasn't sure he should pursue a career as a golf coach, since he had never played professionally before. Because he had told his wife about his New Year's resolution to no longer make decisions based in fear, she was able to remind him of that fact at a critical moment.

It does matter, however, *who* you share with. While it's not always possible to anticipate people's reactions, it's best not to share with someone who is going to undermine your intentions or someone who researchers describe as "lower status"—meaning their opinion isn't that important to you. A set of studies at Ohio State University found that people who shared their goals with someone of lower status were just as unlikely to meet them as those who kept their objectives to themselves. "In most cases you get more benefit from sharing your goal than if you don't—as long as you share it with someone whose opinion you value," Howard Klein, lead author of the studies, concluded. "You don't want them to think less of you because you didn't attain your goal."[24]

This is also a good place to draw on that self-knowledge you have been developing throughout this process and consider what you need most to get and stay motivated. You may remember the story about quarterback Tom Brady (Chapter 1), who discovered that some of his teammates were motivated by shout-outs and positive reinforcement while others, like wide receiver Julian Edelman, wanted to be challenged to do better. We are not all the same and we do not have the same motivational needs, so remember that as you consider who to confide in. A seasoned writer we once heard about used to share all her rough drafts with two people. She called them her angel and her devil. The angel was always very complimentary and supportive, so the writer would always talk to her first for the confidence boost she needed to keep going. Then she would talk to her devil—so called because of the old saying that "the devil is in the details"—who would give her detailed feedback about her pieces that the writer would use to make them better before publishing them for a wider audience.

So what would resonate most for you? Ask yourself what you really need to sustain your motivation.

TAKE CHARGE ACTION:
Share Your Intention

1) Identify *at least* one person you can confide in about your SBT. Consider the research on this subject, as well as your self-knowledge, and make sure to choose someone whose opinion you truly care about and who is likely to be motivating to you personally.

2) Reach out today and ask the person to check in with you regularly about your progress as you work toward your SBT.

A Word about Procrastination

We all have the tendency to procrastinate at some point or another. In fact, according to Dr. Piers Steel, an expert on the subjects of motivation and procrastination, 95% of people admit to sometimes putting things off.[25] (And one has to wonder if the other 5% lack self-awareness or are simply not being truthful!)

Procrastination is often thought of as a time-management or willpower issue, but research suggests it's more often an emotion-management issue. Some of the most common reasons people procrastinate are:

1) Confusion: You are not clear about what you need to do or how to do it.

2) Discomfort: What you need to do feels scary, boring, difficult, or unpleasant in some way that makes you want to avoid it.

3) Distraction: Perhaps because you are feeling confused or uncomfortable, or simply because of the overstimulated way in which most of us live our lives today, what you need to do gets lost or buried under a mountain of other things.

The exercises and tools we have given you throughout this book are for just these sorts of situations. Find yourself confused or lacking clarity about what to do? Go back to Chapter 1 and make sure you have defined a clear and purposeful SBT. Or, return to Chapter 4 to remind yourself of the roadmap you started that shows you how you're going to get there.

Feeling uncomfortable about your ability to get the job done? Return to the mindset tools you learned in Chapter 2 to bring awareness to what you are feeling and build your belief by reframing it in a way you can work with.

Throughout this book, we have tried to help you focus on the things that will move you forward, and that focus should help minimize distractions. Of course, we all know that we live in a highly distracting world, so if you are still feeling distracted, set some ground rules for yourself like the ones that follow. Even if you don't feel distracted, these tactics are good ones to adopt to ensure you're continually working toward your destination.

- Make a commitment to yourself: "The first thing I do in the morning will *not* be to look at my phone."
- Instead, spend your first five minutes every morning visualizing your SBT and the feeling you want to have from achieving it. Then choose three things you can do to move in that direction.
- Block out on your calendar a regular time each week to focus on your SBT, track your progress, and add to or reassess the roadmap that is taking you there.

Again, these tactics work best if you put them in place *before* you need them. The more you can avoid the feeling of procrastination, the better off you will be. Of course, that's not always possible, so the following tip will help when you find yourself already in a procrastinating state of mind.

SELF-COACHING TIP: This tip is called The Five-Second Rule, and it's adapted from a bestselling book of the same name by Mel Robbins. It's pretty simple: If you notice yourself procrastinating, then you must act on what you're procrastinating about within five seconds. Count 5-4-3-2-1-GO! And then start doing whatever you have the instinct to do first. Jason uses this rule when clients have trouble getting started. For example, if someone can't decide how to start their day—should I do my workout or have breakfast first?—he tells the person to choose the first thing that comes to mind and just start doing it. Not only does this help move them past procrastination, but it also helps build momentum—because action tends to lead to more action!

Accept Failure and Setbacks

One of the biggest barriers to sustained motivation is the setbacks we all face along the way. When something unexpected happens or we feel like we have failed, it's easy to feel like we just can't do it so why keep trying. But the path to pursuing a big dream or faraway destination isn't about getting everything right on the first try. It's about trial and error, figuring things out, and making adjustments along the way—and continuing to do so until you get where you want to go.

One of the best things you can do for yourself is to admit upfront, right now, that setbacks *will* happen. It's inevitable. Life isn't static, so even when you master something, there will still be new obstacles to come. That's just how life works in any field, in any industry, in any context, at any time, for any and every person out there. You can spend your time and energy wishing it weren't so or fighting against it. Or you can accept setbacks as a given and the next one as just another opportunity to coach yourself through it and become more resilient in the process. As Jason likes to tell his clients, "There's no such thing as failure, only experience."

Jason saw a stark example of this when one of his clients, Tony Amezcua, a pitcher in the Mexican Baseball League, lost sight in one of his eyes due to a detached retina. The two had already been working together when it happened, and they had developed a process that helped the pitcher build belief in himself, get into a neutral state so he could quiet his mind on the mound, and visualize each pitch before he threw it. That had been working well for him before he got the news that he would need surgery on his eye.

At first, Amezcua wasn't overly concerned about the surgery. This had happened to him before. Surgery had restored his vision then, and he had been able to come back afterward to continue playing professionally. He kept himself busy while he was recovering by continuing to visualize his pitches, running them on a loop in his mind until he could get back on the mound.

But that didn't happen as quickly as he would have liked. It turned out he needed a second surgery, and then a third. After that, he was told the vision in that eye was gone for good.

When he called Jason to tell him about it, he thought his career was over. "Who is going to want a one-eyed pitcher?" he wondered. Jason told him that he understood his concerns, but he thought Amezcua was getting ahead of himself.

"What do you mean?" Amezcua asked.

"Well, you're just assuming that you won't be able to pitch as well as you did before and that no one will give you a chance to try. You don't *know* that yet. In fact, you'll never know it until you try. So why don't you just try and see what happens?"

Jason suggested Amezcua simply work the same process he had been working, and apply it to this new challenge. So that's what he did. Pitch by pitch, he rebuilt his belief in himself and his capability as a pitcher in the exact same way he'd built it in the first place. And then, game by game, he showed his club that he could still win.

It worked. Amezcua called Jason after the season ended and told him it had been one of the best of his career.

It's important to remind ourselves when we hit a roadblock like Amezcua did, or even when we outright fail, that it isn't the end of our story. Maybe we will need to pivot, or just pick ourselves up and try again, but either way, just because something didn't turn out the way we wanted it to doesn't mean that it never will. It just means that it hasn't happened *yet*.

When new obstacles arise, always remember that you have a process here you can go back to. You have exercises and tools you can use no matter what comes up. Remind yourself of that when you start to get ahead of yourself or when you feel like giving up.

Remember Your Wins

One day David was playing at the Seminole Golf Club in Florida with Hall of Fame golfer Raymond Floyd, who counts among his successes sixty-three PGA Tour wins and four Majors, including the 1976 Masters. Floyd was having an okay day, but he wasn't playing a great game. Still, David knew what a fantastic golfer he was, and he's always been interested in how successful people have achieved their success, so around the twelfth hole he asked him a question.

"When you were winning all those tournaments at the height of your career, what were you thinking?"

Floyd thought about it for a moment, and then he replied, "I saw every shot I hit before I hit it, and wherever I pictured it going, that's where it would go."

David thought that was an interesting answer. But even more interesting was how Floyd's game changed after that. On the thirteenth hole, he nearly hit a hole in one. On the fourteenth, he got within a few feet of the hole and then made a birdie. He did just as well on the fifteenth. And then the sixteenth. In the end, he got four birdies in a row, and none of them were easy holes. Conditions were windy that day, and they were playing a tough course.

Afterward, David asked him how it happened—how had he managed to up his game for the last four holes?

"It started with your question," Floyd said. "It got me thinking about how I used to approach shots when I won the Masters and then I started playing like that."

It was a lesson David took with him. Sometimes the best thing to do when we're struggling is remind ourselves of when and how we succeeded in the past. This doesn't just work when reminding ourselves of something tangible, like the mechanics of hitting a good golf shot, but also those intangibles we need to break through—like those times when we found the resilience to pick ourselves up and keep going or the courage to put ourselves out there and try something new.

Dawn Sweeney, president and CEO of the National Restaurant Association, often remembers a time very early in her career when she had the courage to speak up for what she believed. She was working for a company that was going to launch an ad campaign for the USDA to help increase milk consumption among young women in the 16–24 age group—a demographic that was drinking milk less and less. "If that became a trend that played out through their lifetime, milk consumption overall was going to drop precipitously," Sweeney explained, "so we were trying to really arrest that decline and make drinking milk more cool, fashionable, fun, [and] accepted among these young women."

Several different campaign concepts were developed, which Sweeney's boss presented to the Board of Milk Processors. Among the options was the now-famous "milk mustache" campaign that became iconic in the 1990s. But that wasn't the option the Board chose. Sweeney, who was about twenty-five at the time, was sure they were making the wrong choice. She looked around and noticed the board was entirely comprised of men over the age of fifty. This was who was deciding what would speak to young women. As she described what happened next, "I somehow found the—I'll say courage, or audacity, or whatever you want to call it—to say, 'I think I'm the only person in the room that's in this demographic or close to it [and] I honestly think you're wrong.'"

She went on to explain why she believed the milk mustache campaign was the better choice, and eventually, after lots of discussion, they came around. Not only did it prove to be very successful in terms of reversing young women's milk drinking habits, but it was extended to other demographics as well. That one campaign did a lot to advance the industry as a whole during that era, and it might never have happened if Sweeney hadn't spoken up.

We all have triumphs—moments when we won something, got what we wanted, or navigated our way through trying times. When we hit a roadblock or find we're not performing our best, we can return to those past successes and remind ourselves that we can—and have—accomplished big things before. That can provide us with courage and inspiration we need to keep going. After all, if we succeeded in the past, then what's stopping us from doing it again now?

TAKE CHARGE ACTION:
Create Your Personal Highlight Reel

We all know the setbacks are coming, even if we don't know yet what they will be, so why not start remembering your successes now? We call this your personal highlight reel, which is a kind of catalog of life's most successful moments that you can turn to when you need them. They can serve as motivation, proving that you are capable of doing big things, or as education, providing insight about what your thought process was, what worked, and what didn't when you succeeded before—or both!

1) Write down a list of successes you have had in your life. You can do this in one of two ways. You can simply write them down in the order in which they pop into your head, or make

a timeline cataloging your successes from childhood all the way to the present day. They can be big things, small things, or anything in between. The list can be as long as you like. Keep writing as long as the inspiration lasts.

2) Once you have made your list, pick one success and expand on it. Write down the details of what happened and what you did that contributed to that success. Recall any roadblocks you hit and how you moved past them. Once you have done this, move on to another item on your list and do the same—again and again for as long as you want or need to.

3) When you have finished, tag these pages for easy reference. You might even copy them and put them in your desk drawer or somewhere close at hand. That way, the next time you encounter a roadblock on the way to achieving your SBT, or really any time when you encounter difficult circumstances or your belief in yourself wanes, you can take out your list and remind yourself of all the great things you have already accomplished as proof of what you're capable of.

SELF-COACHING TIP: Having trouble remembering your personal highlights? Some of us just aren't wired to think of ourselves in this way, so ask someone who is! Maybe a parent, a partner, or a best friend. Ask the person what they think your biggest successes have been in life, and then let them talk—even brag—about you. Then don't forget to write down what you heard so you can remember them yourself the next time.

Growing from Failures and Setbacks

You surely remember the reframing technique from Chapter 2. We have used it a number of times throughout this book, including in terms of how we view failure. We have said this before, but it's worth repeating here: We must always remember that our setbacks and our failures are our greatest teachers in life. Without them, we wouldn't have been able to learn, grow, and succeed in the ways that we have. As painful as it might be in the moment, every time that we stumble we should reframe that moment in our minds, not as proof that we aren't capable, but as an opportunity to learn and grow. Then we must look for the lesson.

Becky Frankiewicz, president of the ManpowerGroup North America, once told David about what she called "a significant failure" early in her career that she still thinks of to this day. The company she was working for was launching a new product, and she felt strongly about how it should be done. She had a vision for it and had done her homework, so she felt certain that she had come up with the best launch strategy. But there was someone a couple levels senior to her—a woman whom she respected a great deal—who listened to Frankiewicz pitch her strategy and responded in a way that left her feeling deflated. "Why would you suggest doing it that way?" the woman asked her. "That's not the way to do it at all."

Frankiewicz was so disheartened by the response that she gave in without a fight. As she described it: "I knew I was right, but I was so taken aback … that, in the moment of courage, I failed."

It's a lot like the story we told about Dawn Sweeney earlier in this chapter, but with the opposite outcome. One was a positive memory, the other a negative one, but both women never forgot the experience. Frankiewicz got proof that she should have spoken up not long after when a competitor launched a similar product the same way she had envisioned—and to great success. You might think she's been kicking herself ever since for missing the opportunity, but actually she's grateful. Yes, *grateful*.

"Now that I look back on that, I'm so grateful it happened early in my career," Frankiewicz said. "I'm not sure I would have won the battle anyway, but the real issue is that I didn't fight hard enough." It was an experience she learned from and has taken with her. "I've made that mistake once in my career, and I will never make it again."

Sometimes the lesson you take from your setbacks or failures will be about how to do things differently in the future, but other times it will simply be about your own capacity for strength and resilience—and that's okay. In fact, that's more than okay. Those are often the most profound lessons of all. Because let's face it: It can happen that the business you start will fail, or you will get fired or let go from the job you always wanted, or you will get knocked down in some other way that feels like you can never get up again.

Jason once worked with a client named Matt, who was an airline pilot and avid golfer. They met because Matt wanted to improve his putting, but what he learned from Jason became useful in some unexpected ways. Matt was on a snowmobiling trip in Michigan when he was the first to come upon the scene of an accident. He had been happily zipping along when he suddenly saw this flash of black and yellow out of the corner of his eye, so he skidded to a stop and backed up. That's when he saw it: another snowmobiler had crashed hard into a tree. The vehicle was totaled, and the guy was in really bad shape. Matt rushed over to perform CPR. The sheriff showed up soon after with a defibrillator. Nothing worked. The man died at the scene.

After that Matt was in shock. He kept asking himself how this could have happened. The patch where the guy had crashed was perfectly straight. Had a deer run out into his path? Had he been drinking? Had he just lost control? Matt's mind spun with possibilities, but none of it made any sense.

Afterward Matt went back home and back to his work as a pilot. About a month later, the symptoms started. He described feeling this sense of heat across his chest, like he had just applied Vicks VapoRub. His eyes would twitch. He had trouble sleeping and would be woken up by these recurring dreams where he would replay the accident over and over again.

That led to a series of doctor visits before Matt was finally diagnosed with posttraumatic stress disorder. He didn't want to take medication for it because that meant he would be grounded and not allowed to fly. But after trying different therapies without improvement, he finally decided he had to.

It was a difficult time, but Matt was determined to get back into the pilot's seat. In addition to the medication, he turned to meditation and to some of the techniques he had learned from Jason. They helped him to become more aware and accepting of whatever his mind was focused on in a given moment. He learned how to calm his nervous system and get into a neutral state. And he was able to shift his awareness to the place where he wanted it to go. When he would wake up in the middle of the night with anxious thoughts running in his head, he had tools he used to return to a state where he could close his eyes again and return to sleep.

It took some time of course, but eventually Matt was able to get off medication and back to flying. It was one of those things in life that came out of nowhere, but Matt learned that he could find his way through it. It's a lesson we could all use when we find ourselves up against truly difficult circumstances. You never know just what you are capable of until you're tested. And it's often in those most trying moments that real growth comes.

Keep a Flexible Mindset

One of the advantages of reframing failures and setbacks in a productive way is that it allows you to keep a flexible and creative mindset, rather than getting stuck in ideas of how you think things should be or how they should go. Things are going to happen along your journey that will cause you to question some of your ideas or reassess your path. That's okay. One of the main things we hope you take from this book is the idea that no matter what happens, you can choose how you react to it. And your ability to choose a positive course that will move you forward instead of keeping you stuck has a lot to do with how well you prepare yourself for the journey—which is what this process is all about.

Ajay Banga, executive chairman of Mastercard, has talked about how the environment he came from taught him how to stay flexible and adaptable. He grew up in India, in an area where the infrastructure wasn't always reliable, and because of that, he said, "The first thing you learn for everything [is] you've got to have a plan B *and* a plan C." For example, when running a restaurant, "You can be assured that the power will go off when you don't want it to go off. You can be assured that the system to get water to you will not work."

You can't control things like that—which is the case with so much of what we face in life—but you can prepare yourself to take each situation as it comes and use your tools to work through it. This is why in Chapter 4, we didn't create a complete and detailed roadmap to your destination and have it laminated or set in stone. It's a work in progress, and that's the way it should be. That's the way it *will* be all along the way, until you find you have reached the place where you want to be.

This is true even when the setbacks you face are of your own making. Mistakes will happen, but the process of course correcting is the same whether you caused the situation or not:

1) Awareness: Notice that you have gone off course.

2) Neutrality: Keep a neutral frame of mind as you assess what happened and what can be done, rather than blaming, getting stuck, or otherwise misusing your time and energy.

3) Purpose: Remind yourself of where you want to go and why.

4) Process: Use your tools to course correct, to move in a more purposeful direction.

Sometimes our whole lives can even change unexpectedly, and that can affect our destination too. Throughout his career, "food, marketing, and people" were David's sweet spots, the things he pursued because they brought him joy. Focusing on those things helped him work his way up to the position of CEO. That is, until a health challenge changed his focus.

It started with a conversation he had with a former Yum! Brands franchisee named Jamie Coulter. They hadn't seen each other for a while, so David asked Coulter what he'd been up to. That's when Coulter told him he'd had breast cancer. At the time, David didn't realize men could get breast cancer, but the conversation came back to him later that year when he felt a pebble-sized lump near his left nipple. If it hadn't been for Coulter, he might have ignored it, but instead he went to one doctor, and then another, to get it checked out. Both said it was benign.

It was a moment for some self-coaching. David listened to his instincts, which told him something wasn't right, and decided to follow up. And it's a good thing that he did, because if he hadn't, he might not have survived. He went for a mammogram and an ultrasound, which showed that not only did he have breast cancer, but he had a stage 3A tumor, which is the fastest-growing kind you can have.

All of a sudden, getting through his illness and getting healthy became David's new SBT.

He decided he was going to do whatever he could to give himself the best chance of living and living well. He began by relying on his skills as an avid learner to find out as much as he could about what he needed to do. He got advice and support from people he knew. He read everything he could get his hands on that could help. When he read about how Lance Armstrong worked out twice a day while undergoing chemotherapy, David decided to do that, too. Even when he didn't feel great, he would work out before and after treatment. He even entered golf tournaments during that time to help him stay active. He had fun and nearly won a couple.

David decided that he needed to keep active mentally and spiritually as well. He retired from his position as CEO of Yum! Brands, but that didn't mean he wanted to sit on the couch all day. So, while still undergoing chemotherapy, he decided to start a new company—or, to paraphrase the highly prolific author Ken Blanchard, he didn't *retire*, he *refired* by starting something new. [26]

When he came out the other side, some of his values had changed but not his purpose. Food and marketing weren't big drivers anymore, but people still were. So he focused his efforts at his new company, David Novak Leadership, on helping people become better leaders so they could build a better world.

It was all part of his new SBT, which was to do everything in his power to keep moving, keep healthy, and give himself the best chance possible of living his best life. He now has a new picture up in his office that he looks at for inspiration and motivation—this one of himself with a bald head from his chemo treatments that appeared in *People* magazine. It's a testament to his ability to accept what life throws at him, stay flexible and engaged, and be able to coach himself to do pretty big things, even when life presents challenges that can't be ignored.

It was the times that I was in a role that made me feel the most uncomfortable or unsure of myself that was really when I was growing the most.

—LYNNE DOUGHTIE, former chairman and CEO, KPMG

Raise the Bar Again and Again

As a last word, we would like to talk about the idea of continuing this process of personal growth long past the day when you achieve your SBT. There's always going to be another peak to climb because growth and success are never-ending prospects. That's why self-coaching is a never-ending process. This is what life is really all about: our efforts to keep raising the bar, challenging ourselves by setting new sights, and coaching ourselves to get better and better each and every day.

This process that you have just coached yourself through, and the actions and exercises you have practiced along the way, are tools that you can keep in your self-coaching tool-kit and use again and again. To continue to set new sights and up your game, go back to the beginning and cycle through these same steps. And then do it again and again and again.

This is what happens with people who are at the top of their fields. This is what happened with David, who rose to become CEO of a Fortune 500 company and then, even after he retired from that role, went on to try his hand at starting his own business, one that went through several iterations before becoming what it is today. Jason, too, set out to become a golf coach because of how much he loved the sport, but along the way he learned so much about coaching that he now coaches athletes in a wide variety of sports, as well as young people, business executives, even a pilot—anyone looking for help in raising the level of their performance.

One of Jason's clients, golfer Justin Rose, has shown him time and time again that the need for self-coaching never ends. Rose works with professional coaches, of course, but even still, when he gets out there on the course and gets ready to make a shot, it's just him and the ball. Even someone in his position, with all the professional support that he has, needs to know how to set *himself* up for success. This was evident when he was competing in the 2016 Olympics in Rio. The final round of play was nail-bitingly close, with no player leading by more than a single shot at any given time. Rose himself hit a couple of errant shots and ended up at an awkward distance on the critical final hole. He could have succumbed to the pressure in that moment, letting the circumstances shake his confidence, but that's not what happened. Jason always says, "Trust the process and the outcome will take care of itself," so that's what Rose did. Instead of focusing on what could go wrong, he centered himself and focused on what he wanted to do. He gathered the information he needed, made a decision about how to approach the shot, and then he stepped up and did what he already knew he could. He hit a great shot—lofting it forty yards to within three feet of the hole. Then came the birdie that won him the gold medal.

Rose used that same mindset and process a few years later to win the FedEx Cup, and he continues to this day to coach himself to up his game. People who are truly successful never stop trying to learn and grow and get better at what they do.

The need for good coaching never ends, no matter what age you are or where you are in your career. The fact that David and Jason formed a relationship just a few years ago by coaching each other in their areas of expertise is a testament to just that.

TAKE CHARGE ACTION:
Raise the Bar Year after Year

In this last exercise, we want to challenge you to continue raising the bar on yourself. David does this every year on January 1 (and has for decades) to help make sure the next year will be better than the last one, and he never fails to find something new he can work toward in the new year.

It's pretty straightforward and entails asking yourself two questions:

1) Who am I today?
2) How can I be even better tomorrow?

David likes to write down his answers on a three-by-five card that he puts on his refrigerator so he can look at it often throughout the year. We encourage you to do something similar. And then do the exercise again next year. And the year after that!

David's Raise the Bar Exercise

Who am I today?	How can I be better tomorrow?
• Experienced coach	Codify learning for others
• Passionate podcaster	Learn from other podcasters
• Focused, heartfelt giver	More spontaneous giving
• Grateful and positive	Continue daily gratitude and Bible readings
• Good reader	At least one good book per month
• Excellent physical condition	Continue daily workouts and rest one day
• Loving family man	More communication, support, and encouragement
• Good golfer	Develop scratch short game; play my best in tournaments

Jason's Raise the Bar Exercise

Who am I today?	How can I be better tomorrow?
• Husband	Manage schedule better
• Son	Love unconditionally
• Brother	Be less judgmental
• Friend	Accept everyone as they are
• Coach	Hold clients more accountable
• Athlete	Create an outlet for playing more sports

Now that you have the knowledge and skills, you can begin to look for and even create self-coaching moments for yourself. You will start to see opportunities all around you to bring some coaching into the moment, help you move through difficult situations, expand your knowledge and capabilities, and grow yourself personally and professionally. You have everything you need to create the life you want. All that's left to do is to create it. The sky's the limit!

A FINAL WORD

Using Your Coaching Powers to Help Others

Tony Amezcua, the baseball player who continued to pitch professionally despite losing sight in one eye, did something interesting after working with Jason. He decided to become a coach himself. In his off-season (he still plays professionally in the Mexican Baseball League), he coaches young people who live in the Los Angeles neighborhood where he grew up and who have a desire to learn the game like he did when he was their age.

Amezcua decided to do this because, as he said, he "fell in love with the [coaching] process" and wanted to pass it on—especially to kids. He'd noticed kids were often being taught to focus on outcomes, the wins and the losses, rather than the process of learning, growing, and getting better at what they do. He now coaches young people ranging in age from nine to twenty-three, and his work has become about a lot more than just the mechanics of the game. For example, Amezcua recently started coaching an aspiring young player whose low self-esteem was obvious from the start. The kid was painfully shy and had difficulty speaking up for himself. In just a month's time, Amezcua could already see the difference. The young player was suddenly walking into rooms with his chin up. He was more open and spoke with more confidence. These are the kinds of things that will benefit that kid for the rest of his life, regardless of whether he continues to play the game.

It doesn't surprise us that someone like Amezcua, who has found his own success, felt compelled to go from coaching himself to coaching others. Being able to help others on their journeys and watch as they find their own way has been the most rewarding part of both our careers. So, as a final word, we want to suggest something that can help you take your success to the next level: *Coach others the way you have learned to coach yourself.* You can get even more out of the coaching skills you have practiced in this book by applying them to more than just yourself.

As the CEO of Yum! Brands, David could cite numerous financial and business successes that characterized his time with the company. But even more important, and certainly more memorable, has been the fact that he has contributed to the development more than twenty people who have gone on to become CEOs of top companies like

Chipotle, Panera Bread, Kraft Heinz, and even the mayor of Dallas. Nothing has given him more satisfaction than having helped so many leaders develop their self-awareness and self-coaching skills to raise their games and reach their potential. Even better, many of those leaders have gone on to build powerful coaching cultures in their own organizations, thereby impacting even more people.

Similarly, Jason has had the privilege of coaching some of the top golfers in the world, including multiple Major champions. He has helped build success for numerous NBA, MLB, NFL, USTA, and Olympic athletes as well. Then there are the college, junior, and amateur athletes, as well as others outside the sports world, whom he has helped to build confidence in their self-development processes and in themselves. Tellingly, Amezcua isn't the only one of his clients who have been inspired to coach others based on what they have learned from him. It's in this way that self-coaching skills can spread to more and more people.

You, too, can have these kinds of stories in your personal highlight reel, and it doesn't even require you to have some sort of formal coaching relationship with the other person. In our personal relationships, in our daily interactions—at home, at the grocery store, in the office, going about our everyday lives—we can always find moments when we can be more present with the people around us and react to situations in more productive, and more empowering ways. We can do this if we make the conscious effort to be more aware more often, and bring our coaching skills to bear in those moments.

We believe that success carries with it an obligation to help others. But it's a lot more than just an obligation—it's a privilege. We think you will find that sharing what has worked for you, and watching others use it to succeed, is one of the most profoundly satisfying things you can experience in life. Success in your field of choice is great, but there's no better feeling than being able to make a positive difference in someone else's life, especially when you get to do it day after day after day.

When we look back on our careers, these are the moments we remember most and that bring us the most joy—not our own successes, but those moments when we have helped other people achieve something big or do something they never thought they could do. Knowing how to coach yourself is invaluable for your own growth, but it is also the first step in being able to provide wisdom and inspiration for others to succeed.

As you *take charge of you*, we offer you this challenge: Use what you have learned in service of others. As the leader and orator Booker T. Washington once wrote, "The happiest people are those who do the most for others; the most miserable people are those who do the least."[27] Choose to be someone who does the most for others—you won't regret your efforts.

YOUR SELF-COACHING TOOLKIT

The following is a list of the tools you can find in this book. You can also go to **takechargeofyou.com** to find these tools and additional resources online.

Introduction to Self-Coaching: Becoming the Best *You* You Can Be

- Get Ready to Coach Yourself (pg 16)

The Self-Coaching Conversation: Ask Yourself Some Key Questions

- Find Your Joy Blockers (pg 29)
- Find Your Joy Builders (pg 35)
- Discover Your Single Biggest Thing (pg 40)
- Envision Your Destination (pg 48)

The Self-Coaching Mindset: Open Yourself Up to Growth

- Change Your *Nots* into *Not Yets* (pg 64)
- Practice Detachment Breathing (pg 72)
- Put Yourself in a Neutral State (pg 73)
- Shift Your Focus (pg 79)
- Balance Your Negatives with Positives (pg 80)
- Prioritize What You Value Most (pg 85)
- Define Your Purpose (pg 87)

The Self-Coaching Plan: Uncover Transformational Insights

- Make Your Journey a Purposeful One (pg 97)
- Practice Your Humility (pg 103)
- Consult Your Assistant Coaches (pg 109)
- Kickstart Your Learning Curve (pg 118)
- Identify How You Handle Roadblocks (pg 125)
- Listen to What Your Single Biggest Thing Is Telling You (pg 127)

The Self-Coaching Journey: Take Insightful Action

- Turn Insight into Action (pg 141)
- Start Your Roadmap (pg 146)
- Track Your Progress (pg 154)
- Appreciate Yourself (pg 159)
- Flip the Script (pg 161)

The Self-Coaching Habit: Commit to Constant Improvement

- Build Your Motivational Space (pg 171)
- Choose How You Want to Feel Today (pg 174)
- Share Your Intention (pg 178)
- Create Your Personal Highlight Reel (pg 187)
- Raise the Bar Year after Year (pg 200)

ACKNOWLEDGMENTS

It's been an absolute pleasure to be able to write this book together. Our passion is to help others achieve their potential, and we hope this book does just that.

The number-one person we'd both like to thank is Christa Bourg, who helped us write this book. Christa not only captured our thoughts; she helped develop our self-coaching toolkit and simplified our thinking into an actionable game plan. She is the consummate professional, wicked smart, adds so much value, and is a sheer delight to collaborate with. We know we could not have written this book without her. Thank you, Christa!

Both of us are also greatly indebted to our wives, Wendy Novak and Elizabeth Goldsmith, who provided valuable input every step of the way. We would like to thank the David Novak Leadership team, especially Ashley Novak Butler, who did the same. We would also like to thank Rohit Bhargava and the team at Ideapress Publishing for all their help in bringing this book to you.

Finally, we'd like to thank all the people we reference in this book and so many more who have given us their time, care, and experience, which has helped us hone our coaching skills over the years. It's our honor to share them with you.

Thank you for buying this book. All the authors' net profits from this book will go to our non-profit charity David Novak Leadership and will be used to make the world a better place by developing better leaders.

ABOUT THE AUTHORS

Jason Goldsmith was about to turn forty years old when he found himself at an interesting crossroads. At the time he had only had two jobs, one in the military and the other as director of operations for San Diego Harbor Excursions (SDHE). Although he would consider both careers success-ful, as he approached his twelfth year at SDHE, he knew that he needed to make a change.

Jason had discovered golf when he was in the military and knew that he wanted to do something related to the game, but he didn't have a golf pedigree and certainly had no experience in the industry, other than playing regularly with friends. He wondered often why anyone would hire him for any career in golf. As the weeks passed, he continued to ponder how he could possibly get into the golf industry with no experience. He had no idea where to begin and was about to give up when his wife encouraged him to start learn-ing about the industry. Within a few weeks, he had enrolled in a two-week program at the leading club-fitting school in the United States. From there, he became a certified fitness trainer, a certified club fitter, a certified health coach, and he invented a patented alignment aid for putters. He sold high-end custom putters and became a leading putting and green-reading instructor. After just a few short years, he was invited to coach his first PGA Tour client, Henrik Stenson, who he worked with at St. Andrews in preparation for the Open Championship. Stenson took third that year and has been a kind supporter ever since.

As the founder of Goldsmith Performance, Jason has worked with hundreds of junior, amateur, and professional golfers at many of the most exclusive clubs in the world. He has coached multiple Major champions and numerous top-fifty golfers. His accomplishments in golf include assisting Jason Day and Justin Rose in achieving the number-one world ranking, and helping Rose win both the gold medal at the 2016 Olympics and the 2018 FedEx Cup Championship. In recent years, his practice has expanded into other sports including the NBA, MLB, NFL, and USTA, as well as U.S. and British Olympic athletes and coaches, Division I and II college athletes, nationally ranked juniors, and Fortune 500 executives. He is also the president and cofounder of Mustard, a computer-vision-enabled social platform that is revolutionizing human performance coaching by creating proprietary CV/AI technology in partnership with legends Dr. Tom House, Mia Hamm, Drew Brees, Nolan Ryan, Anson Dorrance, and several other Hall of Fame coaches and athletes.

From Jason's very first day at club-fitting school to his most recent coaching engagement, he has known that he is living his destiny. He thinks often about all of the things that had to happen in order for him to have these experiences, and all of the people who have helped and inspired him along the way. Even on the tough days, he believes that the universe is conspiring to guide him, and his heart is full of gratitude.

● ● ● ● ● ● ● ●

David Novak is the founder and CEO of David Novak Leadership; a digital leadership development platform, and the cofounder, former chairman, and CEO of Yum! Brands, one of the world's largest restaurant companies and home to KFC, Taco Bell, and Pizza Hut. With over 45,000 restaurants, Yum! Brands employs 1.5 million people around the world.

You might think that a career like that started out with some sort of master plan, but David's path has been far from typical for a Fortune 500 CEO. His dad's job as a government surveyor meant his family was constantly on the move, living in a series of trailer parks across the country as David grew up. He didn't go to Harvard Business School or even major in business, as many top executives have. Instead, he enrolled in journalism school at the University of Missouri, where he earned a bachelor's degree.

After college, David took a job as an advertising copywriter, making just $7,200 a year. From there, it was his determination to continually grow himself and follow his passions that led to the next opportunity, and the next one after that. It was more a steady evolution than a well thought out plan as he became an account executive at an ad agency, a marketing executive at Pizza Hut, chief operating officer at Pepsi-Cola Company, president of both KFC and Pizza Hut, and finally CEO of Yum! Brands.

Along the way, his success has inspired him to give back and do his best to teach others all that he has learned. While at Yum! Brands, he created a leadership development program called Taking People with You, which became a bestselling book of the same name. Similarly, his program of recognizing and rewarding people for their work was bench-marked by numerous other companies and spawned a book called *O Great One!: A Little Story about the Awesome Power of Recognition.*

David's desire to make the world a better place by developing better leaders has only grown, through the digital start-up he founded, David Novak Leadership, as well as his family's Lift-a-Life Foundation, Lead4Change Student Leadership Program, Global Game Changers, and The Novak Leadership Institute at the University of Missouri. He also hosts the "How Leaders Lead with David Novak" podcast, serves on the board of directors for Comcast, and is a special contributor on leadership for CNBC.

David has been recognized as "CEO of the Year" by *Chief Executive* magazine, one of the world's "30 Best CEOs" by

Barron's, one of the "Top People in Business" by *Fortune*, and one of the "100 Best-Performing CEOs in the World" by *Harvard Business Review*. He received the 2015 Horatio Alger Award for his commitment to philanthropy and higher education and became a lifetime member of the Horatio Alger Association of Distinguished Americans. He is the recipient of the 2012 UN World Food Program Leadership Award for Yum! Brands' World Hunger Relief effort, which raised awareness, volunteerism, and funds to address global hunger. He also received the national 2008 Woodrow Wilson Award for Corporate Citizenship.

TAKE CHARGE

By reading this book, it's obvious that you want to up your game, and you now have your self-coaching game plan in place and ready to go. If you want to keep learning from David and the best leaders in the world:

- Listen and subscribe to David's top-rated podcast, **"How Leaders Lead with David Novak,"** where he interviews the top leaders in business, sports, and entertainment and shares their tips and insights.
- Take his digital leadership courses, available at **HowLeadersLead.com**, that teach you the specific skills necessary to bring people with you to make big things happen.

Let's make the world a better place through better leadership.

ENDNOTES

1   Schwantes, Marcel. "Why Google's Managers Are So Wildly Successful Comes Down to These 8 Behaviors," *Inc.*, July 27, 2017. Accessed May 29, 2021, at: https://www.inc.com/marcel-schwantes/the-8-biggest-things-that-google-managers-do-to-su.html.

2   Goleman, Daniel. "Don't Write Off the Coaching Leadership Style," LinkedIn, August 21, 2013. Accessed May 29, 2021, at: https://www.linkedin.com/pulse/20130821093435-117825785-don-t-write-off-the-coaching-leadership-style/.

3   Harter, Jim. "Dismal Employee Engagement Is a Sign of Global Mismanagement," Gallup Blog, n.d. Accessed May 29, 2021, at: https://www.gallup.com/workplace/231668/dismal-employee-engagement-sign-global-mismanagement.aspx.

4   Llorente, Victor. "Is It Insane to Start a Business during Coronavirus? Millions of Americans Don't Think So," *Wall Street Journal*, September 28, 2020. Accessed May 29, 2021, at: https://www.wsj.com/articles/is-it-insane-to-start-a-business-during-coronavirus-millions-of-americans-dont-think-so-11601092841.

5   Statista Research Department. "Gig Economy: Number of Freelancers in the U.S. 2017–2028," Statista.com, May 11, 2021. Accessed May 21, 2021, at: https://www.statista.com/statistics/921593/gig-economy-number-of-freelancers-us.

6   Fussell, Chris, Silverman, David, McChrystal, Stanley A, Collins. Tantum. *Team of Teams: New Rules of Engagement for a Complex World* (London: Portfolio/Penguin, 2015). Excerpt(s) from TEAM OF TEAMS: NEW RULES OF ENGAGEMENT FOR A COMPLEX WORLD by General Stanley McChrystal, with Tantum Collins, David Silverman, and Chris Fussell, copyright© 2015 by McChrystal Group LLC. Used by permission of Portfolio,

an imprint of Penguin Publishing Group, a division of Penguin Random House LLC. All rights reserved.

7   Wells, Stuart. *Choosing the Future: The Power of Strategic Thinking.* (United States: Butterworth-Heinemann, 1997).

8   Fetell Lee, Ingrid. *Joyful: The Surprising Power of Ordinary Things to Create Extraordinary Happiness* (London: Little, Brown, 2018).

9   Dweck, Carol. *Mindset: The New Psychology of Success.* (New York: Ballantine, 2007). Excerpt(s) from MINDSET: THE NEW PSYCHOLOGY OF SUCCESS by Carol S. Dweck, Ph.D., copyright© 2006, 2016, by Carol S. Dweck, Ph.D. Used by permission of Random House, an imprint and division of Penguin Random House LLC. All rights reserved.

10 Wittry, Andy. "Kareem Abdul-Jabbar: College Stats, Best Moments, Quotes," NCAA, August 12, 2020. Accessed May 29, 2021, at: https://www.ncaa.com /news/basketball-men/article/2020-05-04 /kareem-abdul-jabbar-college-stats-best-moments-quotes.

11 The Hoops Geek. "The Average Height of NBA Players—From Point Guards to Centers," March 12, 2021. Accessed May 29, 2021, at: https:// www.thehoopsgeek.com/average-nba-height/.

12 Cameron, Julia. *The Artist's Way: A Spiritual Path to Higher Creativity.* (New York: Jeremy P. Tarcher/Putnam, 1992). Excerpt(s) from THE ARTIST'S WAY: A SPIRITUAL PATH TO HIGHER CREATIVITY by Julia Cameron, copyright© 1992, 2002 by Julia Cameron. Used by permission of Tarcher, an imprint of Penguin Publishing Group, a division of Penguin Random House LLC. All rights reserved.

13 Penn State. "Negative Tweets Can Trash TV Programs for Other Viewers," *Science Daily* press release, June 22, 2017. Accessed May 29, 2021, at: https://www.sciencedaily.com/releases/2017/06/170622103809.htm.

14 Franklin, Benjamin. *Poor Richard's Almanack* (Waterloo, IA: U.S.C. Publishing Company, 1914).

15 Eurich, Tasha. *Insight* (New York: Crown Publishing Group, 2017). Excerpt(s) from INSIGHT: WHY WE'RE NOT AS SELF-AWARE AS WE THINK, AND HOW SEEING OURSELVES CLEARLY HELPS US SUCCEED AT WORK AND IN LIFE by Tasha Eurich, copyright© 2017 by Tasha Eurich. Used by permission

of Crown Business, an imprint of Random House, a division of Penguin Random House LLC. All rights reserved.

16   Sinek, Simon. *Start with Why: How Great Leaders Inspire Everyone to Take Action* (New York: Portfolio, 2011). Excerpt(s) from START WITH WHY: HOW GREAT LEADERS INSPIRE EVERYONE TO TAKE ACTION by Simon Sinek, copyright© 2009 by Simon Sinek. Used by permission of Portfolio, an imprint of Penguin Publishing Group, a division of Penguin Random House LLC. All rights reserved.

17   Winfrey, Oprah. "Every Person Has a Purpose," Oprah.com, n.d. Accessed May 29, 2021, at: https://www.oprah.com/spirit/ how-oprah-winfrey-found-her-purpose.

18   "The Professor at the Breakfast-Table," *Atlantic Monthly*, Vol. 4 (1859), p. 505.

19   Zakrzewski, Vicki. "How Humility Will Make You the Greatest Person Ever," *Greater Good Magazine*, January 12, 2016. Accessed May 29, 2021, at: https://greatergood.berkeley.edu/article/item /humility_will_make_you_greatest_person_ever.

20   Corkindale, Gill. "Overcoming Imposter Syndrome," *Harvard Business Review*, March 7, 2008. Accessed May 29, 2021, at: https://hbr.org/2008/05 /overcoming-imposter-syndrome.

21   Isaacson, Walter. *Einstein: His Life and Universe* (London: Simon & Schuster, 2008).

22   Powell, Colin L., and Persico, Joseph E. *My American Journey.* (New York: Random House, 2010). Excerpt(s) from MY AMERICAN JOURNEY by Colin L. Powell, copyright© 1995 by Colin L. Powell. Used by permission of Random House, an imprint and division of Penguin Random House LLC. All rights reserved.

23   Trapani, Gina. "Jerry Seinfeld's Productivity Secret," Lifehacker.com, July 24, 2007. Accessed May 29, 2021, at: https://lifehacker.com /jerry-seinfelds-productivity-secret-281626.

24   Haden, Jeff. "A Surprising New Study Reveals Telling the Right People about Your Goals Means You're Significantly More Likely to Achieve Those Goals," *Inc.*, September 11, 2019. Accessed May 29, 2021, at: https://www.inc

.com/jeff-haden/a-surprising-new-study-reveals-telling-right-people-about
-your-goals-means-youre-significantly-more-likely-to-achieve-those-goals.html.

25   University of Calgary. "We're Sorry This Is Late ... We Really Meant to
Post It Sooner: Research into Procrastination Shows Surprising Findings,"
ScienceDaily, January 10, 2007.

26   Shaevitz, Morton, and Blanchard, Ken. *Refire! Don't Retire: Make the Rest of
Your Life the Best of Your Life* (Oakland, CA: Berrett-Koehler, 2015).

27   Washington, Booker T. *Up from Slavery: An Autobiography.*
(London: Doubleday, Page & Company, 1907).

INDEX